Ready-to-Use LETTERS for Youth Ministry

by Tom Tozer

Group

Loveland, Colorado

Ready-to-Use Letters for Youth Ministry

Copyright © 1996 Tom Tozer

Credits
Book Acquisitions Editors: Mike Nappa and Amy Simpson
Editor: Amy Simpson
Managing Editor: Michael D. Warden
Chief Creative Officer: Joani Schultz
Copy Editor: Helen Turnbull
Art Director and Computer Graphic Artist: Kari K. Monson
Cover Art Director: Helen H. Lannis
Designers: Lisa Chandler and Kari K. Monson
Cover Designer: Diana Walters
Production Manager: Gingar Kunkel

Unless otherwise noted, Scriptures taken from the HOLY BIBLE, NEW INTERNATIONAL VERSION®. Copyright © 1973, 1978, 1984 by International Bible Society. Used by permission of Zondervan Publishing House. All rights reserved.

All other quoted material taken from Phil Barnhart, *Seasonings for Sermons* (Lima, OH: The C.S.S. Publishing Company, 1980) and *The Macmillan Dictionary of Quotations* (New York: Macmillan Publishing, 1989).

Library of Congress Cataloging-in-Publication Data
Tozer, Tom, 1945-
    Ready-to-use letters for youth ministry / by Tom Tozer.
        p. cm.
    Includes index.
    ISBN 1-55945-692-2 (softback & disk)
    1. Church work with youth--Forms. I. Title.
    BV4447.T69 1996
    259'.23--dc20   96-19856
                                                             CIP

10 9 8 7 6 5 4   05 04 03 02 01 00 99 98

Printed in the United States of America.

Contents

Introduction

Why a Book of Letters?

In today's world, accurate and timely communication is vital. I work for a major university. Like any other modern institution, we have interoffice mail, fax capability, and e-mail, an electronic system that links us by computer in the blink of an eye.

All this technology reveals a simple truth: While face-to-face spoken communication is vital, the written word holds a position of priority and prestige. Because people know the importance of completing and reinforcing a message by "putting it in writing," they're willing to invest in the tools they need to make their writing more effective.

I think I know why handwritten and typed messages are still the best attention grabbers: When I receive a memo or a letter—whether tucked snugly and sealed inside an envelope or hidden within a file on my computer screen—I can access it easily any time I want to with the flick of a letter opener or the touch of a button. I can see it, and I can look at it as many times as I want to. It's personal. It beckons me to open it. Its commanding presence represents the opposite of the phrase "out of sight, out of mind." Sitting with an unopened or unread letter staring me in the face is like trying to ignore an unopened Christmas gift.

Because letter writing is gradually becoming a lost art, it may be the most novel, most effective way to communicate: "Wow, a real letter! Quick, read it!"

What Does This Mean for My Ministry?

In youth ministry, as in any kind of ministry, we're charged with the task of relating to people. If we can't do that, we're in the wrong field. It's important that we're able to reach (and reach out to) our young people. A word of thanks, congratulations, or encouragement from us may be the only acknowledgment a young person receives. Putting it in writing means we took the time to make our communication clear and complete. Sure, a pat on the back or a smile is essential. **A note or a letter, though, can be saved and savored.** It can also prolong the positive effects of face-to-face interaction.

In this whirlwind world, where human interaction is often reduced to sound bites and advertising slogans, you and I need to find ways to keep our communication with our young people friendly and effective. This book is my effort to help you do that.

So How Does It Work?

Consider this book a youth ministry toolbox. You're making an important investment in your ability to communicate with the important people your ministry touches. Reach in and use these letters as you would tools: Make them work for you. Their purpose is to make your job easier. It's doubtful that you'll use any letter verbatim. You'll probably want to adapt the form and words to your own specific situation and give it your own touch of warmth. Don't feel, though, that you have to rewrite a letter if it suits your purpose as it is. *Your primary mission is not to be original—it is to communicate.* These letters are yours. Use them word for word or as blueprints to shape your own creations.

This resource is easy to use. Just find the appropriate letter in the book, pop the disk into your computer, make any changes to the letter to personalize it for your own specific situation, then print it out on your letterhead. Send it by e-mail, sign it and send it by mail, or even fax it. You'll save tons of time, and you'll be communicating in a meaningful way.

◆ Add Pizazz to Your Letters!

Sometimes a gimmick may help you get your reader's attention. The following are suggested "grabbers" and "nudges" to make the recipients sit up and notice your messages. Use them when you want to add extra elements to your letters, or create your own gimmicks for added pizazz!

Section 1: Welcome and Outreach

☞So the recipient can keep track of upcoming activities, enclose a small pocket calendar.

☞Enclose a drawing of a bunch of grapes, and write this message: "Come be a part of the bunch!"

☞Put a few visitors badges (or stickers) in the envelope, reminding the recipient to invite a friend to church or youth group.

☞Enclose a stick of gum, reminding the recipient to "stick" with the group for a particular event.

☞Put a toothpick in the envelope, along with a note to someone who has joined your group: "Thanks for picking us."

Section 2: Information

☞Include a piece of string for the recipient to tie around his or her finger as a reminder of important events.

☞Enclose a map of your community, with the location of your church (or another specific place) encircled, encouraging the recipient to come to a scheduled event.

☞Decorate the outside of the envelope with a rubber stamp or stickers that say "FYI."

☞If you're sending the "Parent(s), Here's an Update" letter, enclose some photographs taken at recent youth events.

☞If you're sending the "All About Our Youth Group (to new volunteers)" letter, enclose a slip of paper signed by all the teenagers in the youth group.

Section 3: Thank You

☞Include a homemade gift certificate that reads, "For all your help: Good for one great big hug, redeemable the next time you see me."

☞Include a small glove or a drawing of a hand. Write on it, "Here's my hand of gratitude. Please shake it vigorously."

☞Enclose a picture or a drawing of some army tanks. Write "TANKS!" in big letters on the letter or the envelope.

☞In a letter that thanks a volunteer for his or her help, enclose small squares of wrapping paper. You might enclose a note that reads, "Your help was truly a gift."

☞Make and enclose a certificate that says, "For excellence in going beyond the call of volunteerism."

Section 4: Congratulations

☞Put confetti in the envelope.

☞Include a bunch of gold stars.

☞Clip and enclose an appropriate congratulatory headline cut from an actual newspaper (for example, "Banquet to Honor Local Hero").

☞For a "Congratulations on Making the Honor Roll" letter, enclose enough cash (or a customized gift certificate) so the recipient can buy a jellyroll. Attach a note that reads,

"Because you made the honor roll, treat yourself to a jellyroll!"

☞Enclose a glove or a cutout of a hand, and include a note that reads, "For your recent accomplishment, the group wants to give you a hand!"

Section 5: Special Occasions

☞Enclose a balloon with a small sign attached to it: "Air required."

☞Put a birthday candle in the envelope.

☞In the "As You Leave Home for College" letter, enclose several kernels of popcorn with a note that reads, "Pop only in an emergency."

☞In a "As You Move Out of Your Parents' Home" letter, include a note with the recipient's home phone number and a reminder to him or her to "keep in touch with the family."

☞In a "Happy Birthday" letter, enclose a small piece of foil with a note that reads, "Happy birthday! Look at yourself—you should be proud of what you see!"

Section 6: Encouraging Words

☞Have a letter of encouragement personally delivered along with a clothes hanger and a message saying, "Hang in there!"

☞Enclose a rubber band and a message that says, "Stretch yourself!"

☞Enclose a piece of a tape measure or a ruler along with a message encouraging spiritual growth.

☞Include a paper clip holding a slip of paper that says, "You've got it all together!"

☞Enclose some puffed cereal or popcorn and a message that says, "We're so proud of you—we're all puffed up!"

Section 7: Appeals

☞Place a sticker of a banana on the letter, and write this message: "We're appealing to you..."

☞In a letter asking for free sleeping quarters on a trip, enclose a bunch of small cutouts of the letter Z.

☞Enclose a bunch of dollar signs.

☞In a letter asking for money, enclose a piece of play money and a note that says, "We need the real stuff!"

☞If you're sending a letter asking for free items, make a rubber stamp that says "Free!" and stamp your whole envelope with it.

Section 8: Difficult Circumstances

☞Enclose a copy of your home phone number taken from the telephone book, inviting the person to call you if he or she desires.

☞In a letter of condolence, enclose an appropriate prayer.

☞With the permission of your pastor and/or your youth group, send someone who has lost a job an appropriate amount of money to have a new résumé prepared.

☞Enclose a copy of a page from the Bible with an appropriate Scripture passage circled.

☞Enclose a group photo or separate photos of your young people, telling the recipient, "We're here if you need us."

Using the *Ready-to-Use Letters for Youth Ministry* Disk

1. Make a backup of the *Ready-to-Use Letters for Youth Ministry* disk, and store the original in a safe place. You can copy the contents of this disk to your hard drive, or you can use the disk.

2. Open your word processing program as normal. The files on the *Ready-to-Use Letters for Youth Ministry* disk are in the format of ASCII text. **All special formatting has been removed to allow the files to be used in virtually any word processing program.**

3. Find the letter you want to use in the *Ready-to-Use Letters for Youth Ministry* book. You may want to use the table of contents in the front of the book or one of the two indexes (alphabetical and topical) in the back of the book.

4. In the book, find the disk file number at the top of the page for the letter you want to use.

5. Use either the "open" feature or an "import" feature to bring into your program the file for the letter you want to use.

6. Once the file is inside your word processor, you can add any special formatting (such as boldface and underlining) that you may need. You can also "plug in" the appropriate information in the letter and change the wording of the letter as much as you want to!

7. **Be sure to save the file with a new name to retain the text version on your hard drive or on disk for future use.** If you fail to change the name of the new letter, you will replace the standard letter with the new copy.

8. Please note that if a letter does not look right, you may need to change the default font to a fixed-width font such as Monaco or Courier. Also, you may need to adjust the margins in your word processing program.

9. Print out the letter, or send it via e-mail!

Note: The technical support number for your software manufacturer should be included in your software manual. If you are unable to solve your problem, you can contact Group Publishing, Inc., at (970) 669-3836 and leave a message on extension 4414. A Group Publishing, Inc., representative will respond in a timely manner to assist you.

Welcome
and Outreach

Please Join Us

[DATE]

[NAME AND ADDRESS]

Dear [NAME]:

On behalf of some pretty fantastic youth at [YOUR CHURCH NAME], I'd like to invite you to join our special fellowship that meets on [DATE] at [TIME] at [LOCATION].

[PROGRAM INFORMATION, IF NECESSARY]

The British writer C. S. Lewis once said, "Friendship is unnecessary, like philosophy, like art...It has no survival value; rather it is one of those things that give value to survival."

Come join us! I think you'll discover some really great people who will be interested in meeting you. We're all enriched by meeting new friends and sharing our experiences with each other. Come as you are—no frills, no fronts; just be yourself—and you'll fit in just fine.

I hope to see you at our next get-together on [DATE] at [TIME] at [LOCATION]. Feel free to call me at [CHURCH PHONE NUMBER] if you need transportation.

In friendship,

[YOUR NAME]

First Church   123 Any Street   Your Town, 12345

How About Exploring Christianity?

Community Church
12345 Main Street
Anytown, 12345

[DATE]

[NAME AND ADDRESS]

Dear [NAME]:

Want to go exploring? Come and join others like you who are exploring their Christian faith at [YOUR CHURCH NAME] on [DATE] at [TIME]. They would love to have you join them.

I'll tell you right upfront: The Christian faith is full of wonder and mystery. I still don't understand a lot of it. Every day I ask questions, and I'm not always sure I'm on the right track. So when I ask you to go exploring with the youth group at [YOUR CHURCH NAME], I really mean *exploring*. And we'll all have the chance to share our discoveries with each other.

This isn't an invitation to come and be comfortable. It's a challenge to join us in tackling some difficult stuff. The comfort will come in knowing that we're helping each other discover new things about ourselves and about God. We're helping each other grow.

Come explore your Christian faith with us on [DATE] at [TIME] at [YOUR CHURCH NAME]. Come share your light!

Sincerely,

[YOUR NAME]

Glad You've Joined Us

Your Town Church

321 Church Avenue

Anytown,

54321

[DATE]

[NAME AND ADDRESS]

Dear [NAME]:

Wow—how does it feel to have made my day? I hope you're as pleased as I am that you've decided to officially become a member of our terrific group. You've just made us "terrific-er!"

You've been with us long enough to know what a caring and fun bunch we are. We really do try to reach out to one another—during the bad times and the good. Along with your new status as one of the bunch comes the opportunity to help us help others—to extend a hand to people looking for a place to be themselves.

I'm glad you've joined us. Your presence will make a positive impact on our community. God bless you.

Positively yours,

[YOUR NAME]

Thanks for Visiting

Neighborhood Church 12345 Main Street Anytown, 12345

[DATE]

[NAME AND ADDRESS]

Dear [NAME]:

On behalf of the entire group, let me just say it was a pleasure to have you join us [OCCASION]. We like new faces, and yours brightened the room!

Samuel Johnson said, "I look upon every day to be lost, in which I do not make a new acquaintance." It isn't often that we get the chance to welcome out-of-towners. I hope you felt comfortable and at home, and I hope your return trip was a safe one.

Please keep us in your thoughts and prayers, and when you're in our area again, please know that you have a rest stop here any time.

Thanks again for sharing with us. May God be with you.

Sincerely,

[YOUR NAME]

Glad You Were With Us
(someone local)

[DATE]

[NAME AND ADDRESS]

Dear [NAME]:

It was great to have you join us [OCCASION]. Your visit was really very special, and your presence added to the fun and fellowship. I hope we made you feel welcome enough to come again.

Ralph S. Bourne said, "Friendships are fragile, and require as much care in handling as other fragile and precious possessions."

Please consider us your friends. Come back and warm up the place any time. Thanks for sharing yourself with us.

Warmly yours,

[YOUR NAME]

First Church   123 Any Street   Your Town, 12345

Glad You Attended

Community Church
12345 Main Street
Anytown, 12345

[DATE]

[NAME AND ADDRESS]

Dear [NAME]:

I just want to say how happy I am that you attended [EVENT]. We just love seeing a bright, friendly face like yours. Bring your face back any old time.

Sometimes stepping out takes courage, especially when you're not sure you fit. Take it from me: You fit just fine. As a matter of fact, we try hard to provide as comfortable a fit as possible for anyone and everyone. That's what Christ calls us to be—brothers and sisters to each other.

Now that you've tried us on, I hope you found the fit just right. If not, please feel free to talk to me about it. If so, I hope you'll make us a permanent part of your life and help us welcome others who are also looking for a good fit.

Fittingly yours,

[YOUR NAME]

Hey, Groups, Join Us

Your Town Church

321 Church Avenue

Anytown,

54321

[DATE]

[NAME AND ADDRESS]

Dear [NAME]:

Hey—what are you guys doing on [DATE] at [TIME]? Well, if you're not doing anything special, why not come over to [YOUR CHURCH NAME] and do something with us? Together I'll bet we can cook up something very special!

The youth group at [YOUR CHURCH NAME] would like to invite your group to [EVENT] on [DATE] at [TIME]. We can't think of a better opportunity to get together and celebrate our diversity as human beings as well as our common bond as Christians. To put it in downright neighborly language, we'd like to get to know you better. I'll bet we'll discover the same thing—that we all like to laugh, eat, and have fun (not necessarily in that order).

So we can prepare adequate seating and food service, please call me at [CHURCH PHONE NUMBER] by [DATE], and let me know how many we can expect from your church.

We look forward to a great time. Thanks!

With anticipation,

[YOUR NAME]

Haven't Seen You Lately

Neighborhood Church   12345 Main Street   Anytown, 12345

[DATE]

[NAME AND ADDRESS]

Dear [NAME]:

I'm writing just to say we all miss you, and I'm hoping your absence is only temporary. I want you to know that your presence is important to us; when you're gone, the group truly isn't the same. Let this letter serve as a gentle nudge to you to join us again.

Without prying, I want to let you know that if there's anything we can do to help—even just offer a smile or a friendly voice—just let us know. We'll be here to welcome you back whenever you're ready.

If it's a matter of transportation or a schedule conflict, give me a call, and let's see if we can work something out. Whatever I can do to help you remain an active member of our group, I'll gladly do. In the meantime, you're in our thoughts and prayers. We miss you.

Hoping to see you soon,

[YOUR NAME]

Welcome, New Family

[DATE]

[NAME AND ADDRESS]

Dear [NAME]:

On behalf of the young people here at [YOUR CHURCH NAME], I want to welcome your family to our family. I truly believe that the church reflects the personalities of its people, and together all of us project the image of [YOUR CHURCH NAME] to the community and to ourselves.

The fact that you have made [YOUR CHURCH NAME] your church home lets us know that we're doing some things right—and now that you're part of us, I have no doubt that we'll be able to do those things even better!

In Matthew 4:19, Jesus said, "Come, follow me . . . and I will make you fishers of men." Well, we're thrilled that we "caught" you. I think the fishing expedition works both ways, though, so I'm even happier that you "caught" us—and found us to be a "keeper."

We're glad you're home.

Sincerely,

[YOUR NAME]

First Church   123 Any Street   Your Town, 12345

Information

All About Our Church

Your Town Church

[DATE]

321 Church Avenue

[NAME AND ADDRESS]

Anytown,

Dear [NAME]:

54321

Enclosed you will find an outline of the activities and events that go on here at [YOUR CHURCH NAME]. Please pay close attention to the activities that involve your age group. We try to offer something for everyone. If we don't have something for you, just tell us and we'll add it!

But you know what? The best way to find out what's happening in our church is to come see and hear for yourself. It won't take you long to realize you're among good people who like to have fun. You won't have time to feel like a visitor—you'll be too busy participating!

Who knows? You just may help us learn more about ourselves! Our church is here for you. Come check us out. We think you'll find the temperature here warm and just right.

Sincerely,

[YOUR NAME]

What's Coming Up

(non-attending youth)

Neighborhood Church   12345 Main Street   Anytown, 12345

[DATE]

[NAME AND ADDRESS]

Dear [NAME]:

I'm sending you a calendar of upcoming activities for our youth program at [YOUR CHURCH NAME] because none of these activities would be quite as terrific without your presence. You don't want that to happen, do you?

What we're really asking for is a chance to get to know you better. In the process, of course, you'll get to know us better, too. We just may hit it off and develop a terrific relationship. You know, we're all kind of like the ingredients in an enormous tossed salad: We're all different, but together we create a healthy and enriching dish.

I hope you'll consider adding your own uniqueness to our youth group as these events unfold this year. We'd be delighted to welcome you into the mix. Please give it some serious thought—and I promise I won't bug you.

If you have any questions, feel free to call me at [CHURCH PHONE NUM-BER].

Thanks for thinking about it.

Sincerely,

[YOUR NAME]

What's Coming Up
(regular attendees)

[DATE]

[NAME AND ADDRESS]

Dear [NAME]:

With everyone tugging at you to get involved in this new group and that new activity, allow me to be one more tugger as we head into another season of youth activities at [YOUR CHURCH NAME]. I know you're busy, but I hope you'll put our upcoming activities on your calendar and continue to add your special light to brighten up our group.

I want you to know how much I appreciate your participation. Your unique and special talents add a lot to our youth program. The programs and activities we've planned should be so much fun that none of us will realize how hard we're working.

Englishman Edmund Burke said, "Example is the school of mankind, and they will learn at no other." Your commitment to the group is an example to your peers as we work together to share our faith with others.

Thanks for your involvement.

Sincerely,

[YOUR NAME]

First Church   123 Any Street   Your Town, 12345

All About Our Youth Group

(to parents)

Community Church
12345 Main Street
Anytown, 12345

[DATE]

[NAME AND ADDRESS]

Dear [NAME]:

Some letters are an absolute pleasure to write. This is one of them because I get the chance to brag about our wonderful, terrific, second-to-none youth group at [NAME OF CHURCH].

I've enclosed material that will give you some idea about our group's activities within and outside the church. If you have a son or a daughter who is eligible to be a part of our group, I hope you'll encourage him or her to give us a try. (The information includes the times and locations of our regular weekly get-togethers.)

Our young people at [YOUR CHURCH NAME] are absolutely first-rate. They pride themselves on being part of a Christian fellowship that cares and shares with one another—and that also reaches out beyond our doors to a community in need. It's this kind of wholesome interaction that helps teenagers grow in the right direction by putting their faith into practice.

If after reading through the enclosed material, you have any questions about our events and activities, please feel free to call me at [CHURCH PHONE NUMBER]. You also have an open invitation to visit us during any of our get-togethers.

Sincerely,

[YOUR NAME]

Parent(s), Here's an Update

Your Town Church

[DATE]

[NAME AND ADDRESS]

321 Church Avenue

Anytown,   Dear [NAME]:

54321   With so many activities going on with our youth program, I thought you might want to be brought up to date as to what we've accomplished and where we're headed from here. It's an exciting time for our youth program here at [YOUR CHURCH NAME]. The young people are excited and eager for the next challenge.

You're aware of the activities that have involved your family, but I wanted to give you a summary of events and accomplishments from the last few months. Incidentally, thanks for making so many of these things possible.

[SUMMARY OF SPECIFIC EVENTS, ACCOMPLISHMENTS, AND ACTIVITIES: NAME, DATE, OUTCOME, IF ANY]

It's amazing to look back and see how much ground we've covered. This has been a positive and rewarding year so far for our young people, and I'm proud of all of them for their cooperation and participation. We're looking forward to even bigger and better things.

Thank you for your support. Most of all, thank you for your family. You truly are gifts to all of us.

Sincerely,

[YOUR NAME]

All About Our Youth Group

(to new volunteers)

Neighborhood Church 12345 Main Street Anytown, 12345

[DATE]

[NAME AND ADDRESS]

Dear [NAME]:

First of all, welcome aboard! Your decision to jump into the fray and help us with our youth ministry program is one of the smartest moves you'll ever make. (What did you expect me to say?)

I've enclosed some material that will give you an idea of the kinds of activities we're involved in throughout the year. Read through it carefully, then I'll be happy to answer any questions you might have.

The enclosed material will also show you how much our young people reach out to the community in service to others. Our ministry here would be pointless if we didn't live it beyond our church doors.

Actually, I can tell you much of what you need to know about our youth group in just a few sentences—and I won't exaggerate. Our young people are the best. They care about one another and their church, and they're truly searching for answers to some of those tough spiritual quandaries. It's our task to help lead the way with both words and deeds.

Your role as a youth leader is vital in the church. Our young people will look to you not for all the answers but for guidance and direction along paths to their own discoveries.

Again, welcome! I appreciate your willingness to help.

Sincerely,

[YOUR NAME]

Thank *You*

Thanks for Being Part of Our Group

Community Church
12345 Main Street
Anytown, 12345

[DATE]

[NAME AND ADDRESS]

Dear [NAME]:

Sometimes we just need to do a little housecleaning—you know, pay attention to some of those important tasks we've let slide for a while.

Well, this letter to you is part of my own housecleaning efforts because I've been a little rusty (and dusty) about letting you know how much I appreciate your being part of our youth group.

I believe each person's presence in our group helps make it special and unique. Without you, for instance, our group would be missing everything that makes you who and what you are—your talents, your personality, your humor, your ideas, your likes and dislikes, and even your vocal and facial expressions. Because God made only one of you, the entire group is blessed!

Thanks for the time and energy you give to the group. You mean a lot to all of us and to me personally. Let me boil this down to one phrase: **You're terrific!** (Are you embarrassed yet?)

Thanks for being you and for being with us.

Sincerely,

[YOUR NAME]

Thank You, Area Youth Groups

Your Town Church

321 Church Avenue

Anytown,

54321

[DATE]

[NAME AND ADDRESS]

Dear [NAME]:

Our groups go by different names, but we all have talents and skills given to us by God, the giver of all good gifts. I'm glad we can celebrate our differences that reflect our unique backgrounds and traditions. I'm also thankful that we can work together for Christ.

Thank you for being partners with our youth program here at [YOUR CHURCH NAME]. Your help was invaluable. We want you to know that you can always count on us for helping hands and prayers of support.

We hope you'll always think of us as friends. We're all stronger because of our spirit of cooperation. Let's get together more often!

God bless your group.

In unity,

[YOUR NAME]

Thank You, Parent(s)

Neighborhood Church   12345 Main Street   Anytown, 12345

[DATE]

[NAME AND ADDRESS]

Dear [NAME]:

In case you don't know already, you're one of the luckiest families on the face of the earth! [NAME OF TEENAGER] is such a terrific person, I feel as if I should thank you for sharing [HIM/HER] with me and our youth ministry program at [YOUR CHURCH NAME].

It's a genuine pleasure to know [NAME OF TEENAGER], work with [HIM/HER], and watch [HIM/HER] grow in faith. Of course, it's no secret that a child is a reflection of [HIS/HER] home life. You deserve a lot of credit, and you should be very proud.

Thanks for sharing [NAME OF TEENAGER] with us.

Sincerely,

[YOUR NAME]

Thanks, Volunteer, for Your Help

[DATE]

[NAME AND ADDRESS]

Dear [NAME]:

Christmas came early when you volunteered to join our merry band of youth workers here at [YOUR CHURCH NAME]!

If you were a bunch of packages under my Christmas tree, I'd already know what was in each package: One would contain enthusiasm, another commitment, and still another creativity. Unwrapping the rest would reveal patience, kindness, and persistence.

I want you to know how much I appreciate the gift of you. Your help as a volunteer with our youth program has been invaluable. Your willingness to jump in with both feet has really lightened my load and allowed me to spend more quality time with our young people. In addition, your relationship with the kids has meant a great deal to them and is making a real difference in their lives.

Thank you for being there when I needed a volunteer "professional." (I'm glad you don't charge—we could never pay you enough!) I can't wait to work with you again! Thank you!

Gratefully,

[YOUR NAME]

First Church   123 Any Street   Your Town, 12345

Great Job, Volunteer

Community Church
12345 Main Street
Anytown, 12345

[DATE]

[NAME AND ADDRESS]

Dear [NAME]:

Now you've gone and done it! You were such an incredible helper during our recent [EVENT], you've created a permanent spot for yourself! Congratulations! I don't know how we ever survived without you!

On behalf of myself and all our young people, thank you for all you did to help make the [EVENT] such a great success and a wonderful memory. It's people like you who make it possible for people like me to keep this ministry going full-speed ahead. In fact, you made it so much easier, I'm looking forward to our next activity!

The fact that you're a busy person and you have so many demands on you makes your contribution of time and energy even more special. God has richly blessed you with talent, skills, and a generous heart. We've been the fortunate beneficiaries.

Thank you again.

Sincerely,

[YOUR NAME]

Thanks for Caring, Volunteer

Your Town Church

321 Church Avenue

Anytown,

54321

[DATE]

[NAME AND ADDRESS]

Dear [NAME]:

One of the most wonderful things about our work with young people is that we never know when our influence may make a difference in their lives. An encouraging word from one of us today might bear fruit years down the road in the form of a good decision, a kind word, or a selfless act.

Having said that, I want you to know how important our work is with our young people at [YOUR CHURCH NAME]. More important, I want to thank you personally for being such a special person in their lives. The time you spend with them in an atmosphere of caring and sharing is invaluable—and it is greatly appreciated by me as well as by parents and the rest of the church.

There is no greater way to invest in the future than to spend quality time with young people. On behalf of them, thank you for your gifts of light and love.

Sincerely,

[YOUR NAME]

Thanks for Your Encouragement

Neighborhood Church   **12345 Main Street**   **Anytown, 12345**

[DATE]

[NAME AND ADDRESS]

Dear [NAME]:

Edris Stannus, British ballet dancer and choreographer, once said, "It takes more than one to make a ballet."

It also takes more than one person to lead a program, create enthusiasm, and come up with new ideas. I want to thank you for being one of my greatest supporters and for encouraging me to keep going even when I wasn't sure I was going in the right direction. Your friendship has made my work enjoyable and rewarding.

I think we've been able to make some great positive strides in our youth program here at [YOUR CHURCH NAME]. We're excited, and we're all pulling our own weight. In other words, we're working as partners.

Thanks, partner, for your encouragement and support.

Gratefully,

[YOUR NAME]

Thanks for Your Help

[DATE]

[NAME AND ADDRESS]

Dear [NAME]:

Thank you. Thank you. Thank you. Thank you. Thank you. Thank you. Thank you. Thank you. Thank you. Thank you. Thank you. Thank you. Thank you. Thank you. Thank you. Thank you . . .

Whew! I just can't thank you enough for your help.

So I'll stop and just say that without you, I couldn't have gotten everything done. With your skill and energy and commitment and brains, I've never looked so good!

With one more big *thank you,*

[YOUR NAME]

First Church   123 Any Street   Your Town, 12345

Thanks for Listening

Community Church
12345 Main Street
Anytown, 12345

[DATE]

[NAME AND ADDRESS]

Dear [NAME]:

You probably don't realize it, but you gave me a great big bear hug with your ears. Thank you for letting me air my feelings [DATE OR OCCASION].

You were kind and patient, and even though I didn't expect you to come up with solutions for me, you did anyway! By talking with you and having your understanding ear, I was able to see things more clearly.

In this hustle-and-bustle world, time seems to be our most guarded and precious possession. The fact that you shared some of yours with me makes me feel both good and grateful.

Proverbs 4:7 says, "Wisdom is supreme; therefore get wisdom. Though it cost all you have, get understanding."

Thanks, friend, for your wisdom and understanding. Let me know when I can lend *you* my ears.

Gratefully yours,

[YOUR NAME]

Thanks for Your Gift of Money

Your Town Church

321 Church Avenue

Anytown,

54321

[DATE]

[NAME AND ADDRESS]

Dear [NAME]:

"Every good and perfect gift is from above" (James 1:17a).

I know you could have done a lot of other things with that generous contribution you gave to our program. The fact that you gave it to us reassures us that you have confidence in what we're doing. That's worth even more than money!

Our program is like any other here at [YOUR CHURCH NAME]; we're always begging and borrowing (We try not to steal!), trying to make ends meet when we've reached the end of our dollars. It's people like you, whose generosity is surpassed only by the spirit in which you give, who keep this ministry going. In fact, through your kindness and generosity, you're part of our ministry.

Thank you again for your gift. It will go a long way in helping us help others.

Sincerely,

[YOUR NAME]

Thanks for Your Donation

Neighborhood Church   12345 Main Street   Anytown, 12345

[DATE]

[NAME AND ADDRESS]

Dear [NAME]:

I know it's a cliché, but it's true—we couldn't have done it without you and your generous gift! Thank you, thank you, thank you!

With all the appeals for help these days—at the door, in the mail, and over the phone—it's hard to know who deserves what and how much they deserve. That's why your gift means so much: Through your giving, you acknowledge our hard and good work. That means as much as the donation itself.

We try not to beat on too many doors, but we can't sustain the program entirely on our own. We rely on gifts such as yours to provide that margin of excellence that we try to maintain in all we do with our young people.

Thank you from all of us.

With deep gratitude,

[YOUR NAME]

Thanks for the Use of Your Building

[DATE]

[NAME AND ADDRESS]

Dear [NAME]:

On behalf of our entire group, I want to thank you for allowing us to use your [TYPE OF FACILITY] for our program. The facility was perfect for our needs, and everyone felt right at home.

What made using your facility so special was the manner in which you opened your doors to us. You did so with an attitude of sharing and true generosity. We appreciate your hospitality and the fact that you turned everything over to us with complete trust.

We're anxious to repay the favor. If you're ever in need of anything, please ask us first. Even though space can sometimes be at a premium here at [YOUR CHURCH NAME], if you need some and we find any extra, *it's yours!*

Bless you.

Sincerely,

[YOUR NAME]

First Church   123 Any Street   Your Town, 12345

Thank You, Church Family

Community Church
12345 Main Street
Anytown, 12345

[DATE]

[NAME AND ADDRESS]

Dear [NAME]:

It's been said often and in many different ways that the best way to evaluate a church and its people is to observe how much time, energy, and money they invest in their children and young people. If that's the measuring stick, the people at [YOUR CHURCH NAME] are tops!

The youth program at [YOUR CHURCH NAME] is blessed to have such a loving and supportive church family. You've always been cheerful givers.

It's hard to know where to start when saying thank you. All you members of [YOUR CHURCH NAME] have never hesitated to roll up your sleeves and lend a hand for youth events. You've always been generous with your financial support and your time. You may never know what giving that extra dollar or going that second mile may mean to one of our young people in years to come. Your kindness has no doubt changed lives.

Thank you, [YOUR CHURCH NAME], for supporting our youth program. Because of you, our programs will continue to grow and flourish.

God bless you all.

[YOUR NAME]

Thank You, Community

Your Town Church

321 Church Avenue

Anytown,

54321

[DATE]

[NAME AND ADDRESS]

Dear [NAME]:

How do you thank an entire community for supporting your youth program except to let out a great big *hurrah* for [NAME OF COMMUNITY]?

The young people and their directors at [YOUR CHURCH NAME] would like to thank all the residents of [NAME OF COMMUNITY] for their tremendous support of [EVENT]. It was a whopping success, due in large part to the interest and help of many people in the community.

An old proverb states, "Union is strength." I believe our community is strong because in spite of our individual differences, we come together when things of real worth are at stake. The future of [NAME OF COMMUNITY]'s young people is important to all of us. By investing our time and energy in their well-being, we are securing a future for all of us.

Thank you for coming together in support of our young people.

Sincerely,

[YOUR NAME]

Thank You, Area Youth Leaders

Neighborhood Church   12345 Main Street   Anytown, 12345

[DATE]

[NAME AND ADDRESS]

Dear [NAME]:

British dramatist Noel Coward said, "Work is much more fun than fun." You must have a lot of fun in what you do as youth leader at [NAME OF RECIPIENT'S CHURCH] because you work wonders with those young people. This is evident in their commitment and enthusiasm for all the projects they tackle.

Let me take this opportunity to thank you for your dedication to your job as youth leader at [NAME OF RECIPIENT'S CHURCH]. Ours can be a thankless task at times, and commitment such as yours inspires all of us to reach beyond our grasp and to never give up.

Your young people and your church are fortunate to have you—I pray that they realize it. Blessings and best wishes.

In his service,

[YOUR NAME]

Congratulations

Congratulations on Becoming a Christian

Community Church
12345 Main Street
Anytown, 12345

[DATE]

[NAME AND ADDRESS]

Dear [NAME]:

I'm so happy to welcome you into the community of Christian believers. This is the most important step you'll take during your lifetime.

The process of becoming a Christian really never ends. In fact, I prefer to call the process "becoming like Christ" because (1) this provides us with the ultimate goal and (2) our faith never stops growing. It's a journey: always evolving, changing, and maturing.

Your commitment demands that you set high expectations for yourself and others. Life will not suddenly become easier; if anything, living a Christian life can be incredibly hard. God tests our love, patience, hope, kindness, and generosity, and more often than not, we fail miserably.

As you go through tough times in your faith, you can be sure that others will be struggling right along with you, offering you their prayers and relying on your prayers as well. As a Christian you'll never be alone. Even during the darkest of times, God will be with you.

Again, welcome to a new life. Happy rebirth day!

Sincerely,

[YOUR NAME]

Congratulations on Making the Honor Roll

Your Town Church

[DATE]

321 Church Avenue

[NAME AND ADDRESS]

Anytown,

Dear [NAME]:

54321

Congratulations on making the honor roll! That's quite an achievement.

Your hard work has been rewarded—feels good, doesn't it? I hope you'll continue setting these high standards for yourself. There is so much in life, it seems, that only rates as an "OK" instead of a "Wow!" You're an exception to that. Keep it up, and you'll be a standout next time that college recruiter, employer, or scout comes along.

Let me also encourage you to thank God for your accomplishments. He has gifted you with special abilities. In fact, you're a shining example of his generosity. Give him the credit—he walks with you every day.

Again, congratulations! Keep it up!

Sincerely,

[YOUR NAME]

Congratulations on Your New Brother/Sister

Neighborhood Church   12345 Main Street   Anytown, 12345

[DATE]

[NAME AND ADDRESS]

Dear [NAME]:

I just wanted to wish you and your family well as you welcome another [FAMILY'S LAST NAME] into your home. You know what that means: Now you'll have one more person to compete with for TV control, dessert, and bedroom space!

Life will never be quite the same again. The nights won't be as quiet, and the days will be a lot noisier. But you'll get an up-close-and-personal look at what it was like for your parents when you were brand-new. You just may gain a whole new sense of appreciation for ol' Mom and Dad!

I know you're going to be extra busy as you welcome the newest member of your family into your life. Everyone will have to help out, walk more softly, speak more quietly, come up with new funny faces, and hum tunes to the creak of the rocking chair. I know you're up to the challenge. Frankly, I think you'll make a great big [BROTHER/SISTER].

Congratulations to your family. Bless your happy home.

Sincerely,

[YOUR NAME]

Congratulations on Your Baptism/Confirmation

[DATE]

[NAME AND ADDRESS]

Dear [NAME]:

Congratulations on your [BAPTISM/CONFIRMATION]. This is one of the most important steps you'll ever take along your walk of faith. It includes a promise from you and a promise to you.

The agreement you've made with God is a commitment to a life that demonstrates Christian love and service. Use this commitment to guide you in your faith and to help you set an example for others.

Your [BAPTISM/CONFIRMATION] is also a pledge from your church family. Our participation in this special milestone in your life shows our commitment to help you and to love you no matter what.

Welcome to your new life! We acknowledge your promise to walk with God, and we acknowledge our responsibility to help guide you.

God bless your life.

Joyfully,

[YOUR NAME]

First Church   123 Any Street   Your Town, 12345

Congratulations on Your Graduation

Community Church
12345 Main Street
Anytown, 12345

[DATE]

[NAME AND ADDRESS]

Dear [NAME]:

If I had a noisemaker, I'd bake it! If I had a cake, I'd shake it! If I had your hand, I'd play it!

Now that you're a certified graduate, you should be able to unscramble the statements above and come up with three ways I'm congratulating you on this education milestone. (If you can't do it, I'm not sure you really should be let loose on the world.)

What a great time in your life! You've come to a new beginning, and your hopes and dreams lie ahead. Make the most of it. Aim high. Think big. Now's the time in your life to look through all the windows of opportunity before you. Check your mirror, too: Take some time to get to know yourself a little better. Then choose your course and go for it. Put your own indelible stamp of excellence on everything you touch!

Remember to take God with you. He's helped you get this far—he'll stick with you all the way.

Again, congratulations!

Sincerely,

[YOUR NAME]

Congratulations on Your New Job

Your Town Church

321 Church Avenue

Anytown,

54321

[DATE]

[NAME AND ADDRESS]

Dear [NAME]:

I know there are at least three very happy people in the universe at this moment. You're happy because of your new job. Your new boss must feel lucky to have you on the payroll. And I'm overjoyed because I know how much you deserve a great opportunity like this to prove what you can do. (Actually, *everyone's* thrilled for you!)

Consider your new job as God's way of opening another door to your future. You can't see what he has in store for you, but his plan for your life is gradually unfolding.

This is your chance to put your own stamp of excellence on something. Make your shoes so hard to fill that they'll have to keep you and make it worth your while. Remember, too, that your present job is your best recommendation for your next job. Let your work speak for itself—loudly and clearly.

This is a great accomplishment. There'll be many more!

Sincerely,

[YOUR NAME]

Congratulations on Getting Your Driver's License

Neighborhood Church   12345 Main Street   Anytown, 12345

[DATE]

[NAME AND ADDRESS]

Dear [NAME]:

Congratulations on getting your driver's license! Of course you've driven your parents crazy for years, so you've had a lot of practice!

Seriously, I think this milestone in a person's life provides a wonderful opportunity to remember Christ's commandment to love our neighbors as ourselves. When you're behind the wheel of an automobile, taking care of others can be literally a matter of life or death.

I'm proud of your achievement. You've earned a newly found freedom that will give you much joy. Along with that freedom comes responsibility, though. Take care of yourself and others, and let God be your one constant passenger.

Oh—and always brake for brick walls!

Precautionarily yours,

[YOUR NAME]

Congratulations on Your Job Promotion

[DATE]

[NAME AND ADDRESS]

Dear [NAME]:

Congratulations on your new position with [NAME OF COMPANY/ ORGANIZATION]. Just when we think we'll never go any further than we have, God nudges us by reminding us of our untapped potential. Who's gonna argue, right?

You deserve it. You've worked long and hard to prove your abilities, and now you're getting the rewards. Take advantage of the opportunity and be the best who's ever worked in that position. After all, the ladder of success reaches high, and there are many more heights to reach.

I know you're up to the climb!

We're all proud of you. Remember to give God some credit for your accomplishment. He's gifted you with talents and skills, and now you're returning that gift through your good work.

Congratulations!

Sincerely,

[YOUR NAME]

First Church   123 Any Street   Your Town, 12345

Congratulations on Your Performance

Community Church
12345 Main Street
Anytown, 12345

[DATE]

[NAME AND ADDRESS]

Dear [NAME]:

Here's my critical review of your performance [DATE OF PERFORM-ANCE]—*simply wonderful!*

It was obvious that you put a lot of preparation and perspiration into it because you kept our attention throughout the entire [PROGRAM/PER-FORMANCE]. You did yourself, your family, and your "fans" real proud, and we can't wait until your next performance.

You have a God-given talent, and I'm glad to see that you're using it to the fullest. A talent is kind of like a plant or flower. It needs nourishment and proper care in order to grow. As it matures, it grows in beauty and grace. Your talent will continue to develop and grow as you nurture it. I think God gives you the raw material—it's up to you to take advantage of opportunities to make something of it.

Keep up the good work! And thank you for sharing your talent with us.

Applause! Applause! Applause!

[YOUR NAME]

Congratulations on Your School Award

Your Town Church

321 Church Avenue

Anytown,

54321

[DATE]

[NAME AND ADDRESS]

Dear [NAME]:

Is your wall in your room getting full yet? Well, whether this is your first award or just your most recent one, I think you should consider starting a [LAST NAME OF TEENAGER] "wall of fame" because I'm sure you'll have a huge collection someday. One of these days, you'll be giving tours!

Congratulations on your [DESCRIPTION OF AWARD]. I'm delighted that you received it, but I'm hardly surprised. If we had a wall of fame at [YOUR CHURCH NAME], you'd be on it for sure!

We're all very proud of you. You're an example of someone putting God's gifts into action. Your accomplishment also helps us all to remember where our gifts come from and to be thankful for them. Just think—God puts all the parts together, breathes life into them, and here we are! Yep, he really does do good work.

I'm sure there will be many more awards and honors in your future. Receive them humbly, and always remember to acknowledge the Giver of your skills and talents.

Sincerely,

[YOUR NAME]

Congratulations on Your Sports Award

Neighborhood Church   12345 Main Street   Anytown, 12345

[DATE]

[NAME AND ADDRESS]

Dear [NAME]:

Consider this letter a handshake, a pat on the back, and a hug! Congratulations on your [DESCRIPTION OF AWARD].

By earning this award, you've demonstrated the importance of your athletic skills. Those same skills will serve you well throughout your life—in the class-room, on the job, and in your church. Your award puts you in the spotlight where others will see you and follow your example. That's a big responsibility.

Your friends at church are very proud of your accomplishment. You will have many more honors and awards in your life because you truly are a winner. Keep up the good work, and you'll continue to be an inspiration to others.

God has blessed you with a terrific skill. Continue to use it, sharpen it, and always be grateful for it.

Proudly,

[YOUR NAME]

Congratulations on Your New Responsibilities

[DATE]

[NAME AND ADDRESS]

Dear [NAME]:

Thanks a bunch for agreeing to take on more responsibility in the youth group. I know how busy you are, and I know this wasn't a quick or easy decision for you.

I want you to know that I really need your leadership abilities. Not only do you always get the job done; you see to it that others are getting theirs done. You're dependable, you're on time, and you have this weird knack for excellence. *Do you realize how rare those qualities are?* You have no idea how many gray hairs you'll save me!

God recognizes that you have a lot to do, and he also understands your quest to be the best you can be. Ask him to help you shuffle your priorities so you can do a good job, keep a sense of humor, and focus on what's most important.

God has given you many talents and abilities. That makes us the lucky ones!

Thanks for being involved.

Sincerely,

[YOUR NAME]

First Church

123 Any Street

Your Town, 12345

Congratulations, Parent, on Your Job Promotion

Community Church
12345 Main Street
Anytown, 12345

[DATE]

[NAME AND ADDRESS]

Dear [NAME]:

Wow! It's only a matter of time before you'll be the top dog, the head honcho, the most mighty muckety-muck! With your newest assignment, you're certainly headed in the right direction!

Your new position is really quite a compliment to you because it shows that your employer realizes you're a person who can help take the company to the next level. There is wisdom in surrounding yourself with highly capable people. Your boss is wise in recognizing what you can contribute to the team.

Your church family is proud of you too. It won't take your new co-workers long to realize what we already know—you're terrific! Your accomplishment is a testimonial to the Creator who, when he put the finishing touches on you, broke the mold.

Congratulations to a real one-of-a-kind human being!

Sincerely,

[YOUR NAME]

Special
Occasions

Happy Birthday
(general)

Neighborhood Church   12345 Main Street   Anytown, 12345

[DATE]

[NAME AND ADDRESS]

Dear [NAME]:

Happy birthday! This is the day—oh, those many years ago—that something very special happened in the history of the world: You were born. And believe it or not, since you joined the human race and have run around the track a few times, history has been changed for the better. You didn't know how important this occasion is, did you?

Well, from one history maker to another, let me just say congratulations and thank you for making my world and our world a little brighter with your presence. You're a special and unique creation of God, and I have to believe that God is looking down on you right now and patting himself on the back for a job well-done.

Your birthday is a significant event. Enjoy it!

In celebration,

[YOUR NAME]

Happy Thirteenth Birthday

[DATE]

[NAME AND ADDRESS]

Dear [NAME]:

Wow! Now your age has a "teen" on the end of it—look out, world!

Congratulations on your thirteenth birthday. You're now officially a teenager, with all the rights and privileges that come with it. Let's see . . . a lot of people think being thirteen means you get to turn up your music. According to some, being thirteen entitles you to be just a little more deaf, especially when you "don't hear" things like "[NAME OF TEENAGER], please clean your room, take out the trash, and finish your homework!" A lot of people would say being thirteen also means you can now offer sage advice to those twerpy twelve-year-olds.

Seriously, this is an important stage in your life. You're still learning and growing, and you'll be experiencing a lot of physical and emotional changes. It's all part of growing up.

Always remember to include God in that development process. He's helped you reach thirteen, and he wants to be your partner for life.

Thirteen: What a lucky number after all!

Blessings!

Sincerely,

[YOUR NAME]

First Church   123 Any Street   Your Town, 12345

Happy Eighteenth Birthday

Community Church
12345 Main Street
Anytown, 12345

[DATE]

[NAME AND ADDRESS]

Dear [NAME]:

Oh, I wish I were writing this letter to myself! Let's see… what would I say?

Dear Me:

How lucky you are to be eighteen years old! Life is just beginning for you, and so many choices are ahead of you. Choose wisely but boldly. Take some risks. Do some things now before they become "if onlys." Be the best you can be in everything you do. It's no big deal to be just as good as everyone else—put your own lasting mark on everything you do.

Signed,
Me

Back to reality! Since I'm writing to you with the wisdom of a few years under my belt, let me first congratulate you on reaching this milestone in your life. Second, let me remind you that your journey from here on will be exhilarating, frightening, fun, difficult, and enlightening. Remember to take God with you. The ride will not always be smooth, but you'll have him to steady you.

Happy eighteenth! It couldn't have happened to a nicer seventeen-year-old!

Sincerely,

[YOUR NAME]

Merry Christmas

Your Town Church

[DATE]

[NAME AND ADDRESS]

321 Church Avenue

Anytown,

54321

Dear [NAME]:

Humorist Elwyn Brooks White once said, "To perceive Christmas through its wrapping becomes more difficult with every year."

The point is clear: As Christians we have to work very hard to keep our focus on the real significance of the season in spite of all the holiday hoopla. To help you do that, let me suggest a Christmas commemoration strategy.

First, read the Christmas story in the Scriptures with your family and talk about its meaning for today.

Second, focus on the wonderful gifts that God has given you personally—your faith, your family, your abilities, your intellect, your friends, your teachers, and your freedom to live and worship as you choose.

Third, do those first and second exercises every day throughout the Christmas season. Make this a priority.

Finally, make it a personal goal, after the season is over, to continue doing those focusing exercises at least once a week throughout the rest of the year—until the Christmas season rolls around again.

During this season, as during the rest of your life, there will be a lot of noise and distractions around you. With all the distractions and mixed signals we throw God's way, isn't it wonderful (and incredible) that he never forgets us?

Christmas is a celebration of God's focus on each of us. This year let's really try to return the favor.

With Christmas blessings, peace, and goodwill to you and your family,

[YOUR NAME]

Happy New Year

[DATE]

Neighborhood Church 12345 Main Street   Anytown, 12345

[NAME AND ADDRESS]

Dear [NAME]:

Another year is almost here, and it's always a challenge to know what to say to each other that is new and enlightening. I know we all have some bad habits that we should get rid of. I'm sure there are also some good habits that all of us should develop as we head into [NEW YEAR]. So to start the year off right, let's try to break our bad habits and develop those good ones!

Let me offer a few reminders. First, let's all resolve to keep God first in our lives—to see and acknowledge him in everything we do and in every person we meet.

Second, let's make prayer an attitude in our lives. Rather than making prayer a mechanical activity—often used as a last resort—let's try to live with a prayerful attitude. Remember: Listening to God is 99 percent of what prayer is all about.

Last, in our longing for peace and goodwill among all people, let's first promote those feelings among our friends, family, and co-workers.

I'm looking forward to another year together. Thanks for all you've done and everything you'll do in [NEW YEAR]!

Sincerely,

[YOUR NAME]

Happy Easter

[DATE]

[NAME AND ADDRESS]

Dear [NAME]:

Pastor Phil Barnhart tells of a trip he took to a tomb in Jerusalem: "I saw a plaque that said, 'Enter with reverence. Leave with a smile. He's not here.' "

To me this is what Easter is all about. It's a time of reverence and awe—and because we know that Christ is alive and *lives* in those who know him, we should celebrate with a huge smile.

When we smile at life, people's curiosity usually gets the best of them. They wonder what we're thinking or what we're up to. Do we know something they should know?

Especially during this season, we smile because we *know* we worship a risen Lord and Savior. We also have the responsibility of sharing our joy with others. We're asked to live our faith by both what we say and what we do.

This year, let's celebrate Easter with the smile of realization that we're loved unconditionally and Christ has prepared a place for us beyond the tomb. *How can we not smile?*

May this season's meaning remain alive in your heart.

Joyfully,

[YOUR NAME]

First Church   **123 Any Street**   **Your Town, 12345**

As You Leave Home for College

Community Church
12345 Main Street
Anytown, 12345

[DATE]

[NAME AND ADDRESS]

Dear [NAME]:

It's hard to know if your leaving for college is more difficult for you or your family. I can tell you one thing—those of us who love you sure will miss you.

You're setting out on one of life's greatest adventures—something that's fun and scary at the same time. But it couldn't happen to a nicer person. College will challenge your head and your heart, and you have the head and the heart to handle it.

As you set off on this new adventure, we want you to know that even though you won't be as close to your family and friends as you have been, we'll all keep you close in our hearts and prayers.

Wherever you go, take God with you. And take comfort in knowing that even when you forget him, he'll never forget you.

Have fun. Work hard. Learn. Pray always.

We love you. Go with God.

[YOUR NAME]

As You Move Out of Your Parents' Home

Your Town Church

321 Church Avenue

Anytown,

54321

[DATE]

[NAME AND ADDRESS]

Dear [NAME]:

I'm writing to let you know that if you're kind of sad right now, that will gradually change. Moving away from home is one of those inevitable realities of life. Most of us do it eventually, and it turns out OK.

Reality has a great way of shaking things up so everything seems all wrong at first, then rearranging everything so gradually it seems all right.

Look at this as one of those happy/sad occasions. Everyone will enjoy more privacy—and everyone will be just a little lonely sometimes. The bathroom will be more accessible—but it may seem too available. Meals around the table . . . won't go all the way around the table anymore. (But for you it could be a lot more fun and less messy eating over the sink!)

Remember—enjoy your independence but remain dependable. Don't let "your own space" become your only space. And save some room for God.

Enjoy your independence!

[YOUR NAME]

As You Begin a New Dating Relationship

Neighborhood Church   12345 Main Street   Anytown, 12345

[DATE]

[NAME AND ADDRESS]

Dear [NAME]:

A person would have to be either blind or out of town not to see that you've seemed pretty happy since you've been spending a lot of time with [NAME OF SPECIAL PERSON]. You two seem to be hitting it off just fine. I'm very happy for you both.

It's always wonderful to see a relationship between a guy and a girl start growing. This is an exciting time in your lives when you should learn together, laugh, talk, observe, and get to know the real yous!

Remember to include God in your lives as your relationship develops and matures; it will be important for you both to rely on your faith to give you guidance. Pray for wisdom and good judgment as you both experience the ups and downs of a meaningful relationship.

May God bless your time together.

Sincerely,

[YOUR NAME]

At the End of a Dating Relationship

[DATE]

[NAME AND ADDRESS]

Dear [NAME]:

I want you to know that my thoughts and prayers are with you right now as you're experiencing one of life's real disappointments. I know you're doing a lot of thinking and wondering and second-guessing.

I hope you'll include God in your quiet time. Sometimes our personal worlds are shaken up for no apparent reason at all. During those times, we need to rely on God to help us find meaning and clarity.

You and [NAME OF OTHER PERSON] have your reasons for going your separate ways for now. That's a private matter between you two. It's always possible that this may be just a temporary break and that your time away from each other will be a much-needed time for thinking and healing.

Whatever the case, you and [NAME OF OTHER PERSON] are in my prayers. I will not intrude, but please know that I'm here if you want to talk.

Sincerely,

[YOUR NAME]

First Church   123 Any Street   Your Town, 12345

As You Move Up a Grade

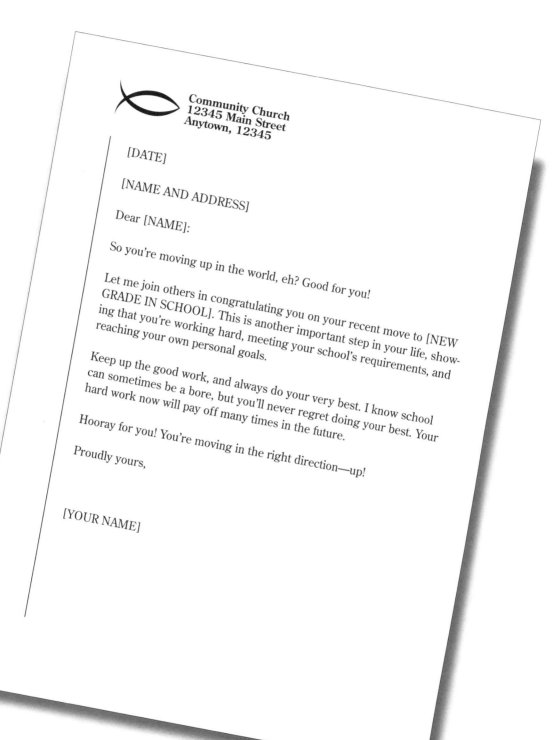

Community Church
12345 Main Street
Anytown, 12345

[DATE]

[NAME AND ADDRESS]

Dear [NAME]:

So you're moving up in the world, eh? Good for you!

Let me join others in congratulating you on your recent move to [NEW GRADE IN SCHOOL]. This is another important step in your life, showing that you're working hard, meeting your school's requirements, and reaching your own personal goals.

Keep up the good work, and always do your very best. I know school can sometimes be a bore, but you'll never regret doing your best. Your hard work now will pay off many times in the future.

Hooray for you! You're moving in the right direction—up!

Proudly yours,

[YOUR NAME]

Here Are the Rules for a Youth Trip

Your Town Church

[DATE]

[NAME AND ADDRESS]

Dear [NAME]:

321 Church Avenue

Anytown,

54321

Before we leave for [DESTINATION AND DATE], it might be a good idea to review some basic ground rules to make sure everyone has a good time. First remember that wherever we go and whatever we do, we're ambassadors for Christ and representatives of [YOUR CHURCH NAME]. People will form lasting impressions of Christianity based on the way we conduct ourselves.

The following behaviors should be practiced only when no one outside our group is watching or listening: (1) making faces when the food is horrible, (2) making disapproving noises because there's just one bathroom, and (3) describing someone else's church basement as a roach motel.

Seriously, common sense is always the best guide to follow when it comes to knowing how to behave. Let that be our most important rule—**Use common sense in every decision and action.**

Here are a few others:

- Respect each other's occasional need for space and privacy while traveling together.
- Remain with the group and pitch in whenever there's work to be done.
- If you need to leave the group for any reason, make sure you let an adult know—**and take someone with you.**
- Think of everything you do on the trip as work on God's behalf. Act accordingly.

[YOU MAY WANT TO ADD MORE SPECIFIC RULES.]

If you're thinking that this letter was totally unnecessary, *good!* That means I haven't told you anything you don't already know—and that means we're in for a great time together!

Thanks for your spirit of cooperation. I'm looking forward to our trip together.

Eagerly and excitedly,

[YOUR NAME]

Before You Go on a Missions Trip

Neighborhood Church   12345 Main Street   Anytown, 12345

[DATE]

[NAME AND ADDRESS]

Dear [NAME]:

Best wishes on your upcoming missions trip! If you feel any butterflies at all, it's only because you're someone who jumps into a project with all your heart, mind, and soul. That's why God chose you for the job.

For the next [DURATION OF TRIP], you'll be God's messenger to that little corner of the world. What you do and say there will affect the lives of many people in ways that you can't imagine. Accept this challenge as a trust from God. He has given you many talents, and now's your chance to use them.

Your entire church family is proud of you. Our prayers will be with you, and we'll eagerly look forward to a full report of your experiences when you return. One tip: I encourage you to keep a daily journal because you'll want to relive this experience many times.

Go with God—and our prayers.

Sincerely,

[YOUR NAME]

Encouraging
Words

Live Your Faith With Your Friends

Community Church
12345 Main Street
Anytown, 12345

[DATE]

[NAME AND ADDRESS]

Dear [NAME]:

I'm writing to remind you of your assignment. This isn't an assignment from me. As a matter of fact, it's my assignment, too: It's the challenge God gave us to share his love with everyone around us.

I know what you're thinking: **"You've gotta be kidding! Everyone? How?"**

I know it's not always easy to live your faith. In your circle of friends, it may not be considered cool. But you know what? Living the Christian faith brings joy, peace of mind, and a growing relationship with God. Wouldn't you like to share those things with your friends?

I don't think we have to preach on a street corner or put down other people's beliefs. I think God calls us to share our faith by living a life that reflects goodness, integrity, and love. If these things radiate from us, we'll be shining examples for others.

OK, start slowly. Next time you're with your friends—at school, at a party, at a movie, wherever—let God's love work through you in what you say and do. Be positive and confident. Allow the joy of being a Christian to shine through you. You may be doing your friends (and yourself) a favor that will last forever!

Joyfully yours,

[YOUR NAME]

Don't Give Up

Your Town Church

[DATE]

[NAME AND ADDRESS]

321 Church Avenue

Anytown,

54321

Dear [NAME]:

Forgive me if I'm trying to be too helpful, but I really feel the urge to write and offer a word of encouragement. It's hard not to be a cheerleader for someone I consider to be a real winner!

Life presents us with so many hurdles to leap over. Sometimes they just seem too high. But usually we aren't limited by the height of the hurdles. We're limited by our own lack of confidence or low expectations of God.

I want to reassure you that I'm cheering for you. So is God. He wants you to use your gifts and accomplish great things in your life. Sometimes he slows us down or changes our direction. Maybe that's what he's doing with you. Pray every day, and listen real hard.

Keep trying and never give up. You have what it takes to make it!

My prayers are with you.

[YOUR NAME]

Everybody Makes Mistakes

Neighborhood Church   12345 Main Street   Anytown, 12345

[DATE]

[NAME AND ADDRESS]

Dear [NAME]:

You know what? A mistake is like a steppingstone. If we're not allowed to make mistakes, we'll stop stepping. You know where that will get us? *Nowhere.*

Your future will take you wherever you want to go. You have the talent, personality, and character to soar to the top! That doesn't mean you won't run into bumps in the road, incredibly high hurdles, and immovable brick walls that will flatten your nose and clobber your ego.

I know you feel bad right now. That's only natural. I also know that you need to put it behind you. No matter how dark things seem today, the future will always bring daylight, and life goes on. As Christians, we are already forgiven. You need to forgive yourself.

You're special. You're loved. And yes, you're human. Hey—the rest of us still have a lot of mistakes to make. Join us. We need to take those steps together!

Sincerely,

[YOUR NAME]

Be Strong in Your Faith

[DATE]

[NAME AND ADDRESS]

Dear [NAME]:

Ah, life! Sometimes we feel as if we can't live with it, and we certainly can't live without it. At times we can feel alone. But through all the fear, the confusion, or the mystery, we always have our faith to keep us going.

It's kind of like keeping the family car maintained so it will always be dependable—or studying hard in school so you're always prepared for a pop quiz. We have to keep our faith well-oiled and in good condition so it will carry us through the best of times and rescue us during the worst of times.

Right now you need to remain strong in your faith. If you feel as if God has abandoned you and you're walking alone, maybe it's you who has lost your grasp on God's hand. He's with you. Reach out, take his hand, and tighten your grip.

I'm praying for you as you travel on your journey of faith.

Prayerfully,

[YOUR NAME]

First Church   123 Any Street   Your Town, 12345

Hey, Junior Higher, Hang in There

Community Church
12345 Main Street
Anytown, 12345

[DATE]

[NAME AND ADDRESS]

Dear [NAME]:

This is a tough time in your life, isn't it? Junior high—the in-between time. You're too young but you're too old, too. You're too tall and too short. You're definitely not old enough to know everything, but you're certainly old enough to know better!

Drives you crazy, doesn't it?

And of course, we older folks have been there, done that—we know how it feels. That always makes you feel better to be told that, right?

You may scream now.

OK, now that you have that off your chest, let me just share a couple of thoughts with you. First of all, make the very best of these years because they'll pass very quickly, and you'll look back on them with fond memories.

Second, at this time in your life, the friendships you form are very special and can last a lifetime. Choose them wisely.

Third, believe it or not, God speaks to junior highers, too! Right now, if you listen real hard during your prayers, God will help guide you through these times of questions, doubts, and lots of temptations.

Keep on keeping on! Even when life seems to be totally unreasonable, completely unfair, and way too tough, remember that you're a unique and totally terrific creation. God always pays attention to what you have to say—even when it seems like others don't.

Hang in there, [NAME OF JUNIOR HIGHER]! And come talk to me any time.

Sincerely,

[YOUR NAME]

You're a One-of-a-Kind Creation

Your Town Church

[DATE]

[NAME AND ADDRESS]

321 Church Avenue

Anytown,

54321

Dear [NAME]:

The only you is you. If that comes as a surprise to you, let me remind you that you're a special creation of God. He didn't use you for practice. He was trying for something unique. And guess what? He succeeded!

I know, I know—in this world of databases and computer printouts, it's easy to feel like just another item on a long list. It can be discouraging and even dehumanizing.

God doesn't want his customized creations to feel unimportant or unloved. Everything you are—inside and out—is everything we're not! When it comes to being you—*you're it!*

I'm proud of you. You should be proud of you too.

Very sincerely,

[YOUR NAME]

Always Give It Your Best Shot

Neighborhood Church   12345 Main Street   Anytown, 12345

[DATE]

[NAME AND ADDRESS]

Dear [NAME]:

Aim high and soar to the top!

Wouldn't it be sad if everyone did just enough to get by? There would be no examples of excellence to follow, no models to look up to. Life would never rise above mediocrity.

Most of us have already been victims of others who just don't care about doing or being their best. It often seems as if quality just isn't built into anything any-more—products, services, even character.

Christians aren't immune to being mediocre, dropping the ball, leaving loose ends dangling, or letting each other down. We can be just as lazy, uncaring, and irresponsible as anyone else.

I want to encourage you to do and be your best in everything you tackle. If you don't leave your own personal mark of excellence on everything you touch, why bother?

Consider this letter a challenge to try your hardest and to do your best. You have a lot to offer.

Soaringly yours!

[YOUR NAME]

Your Spiritual Growth Is Showing

[DATE]

[NAME AND ADDRESS]

Dear [NAME]:

I'm really proud of your growth and development as a Christian. I can see the confidence radiating in your face. I can feel the warmth of your heart as you reach out to others. And I'm also pleased that you continue to search, probe, and ask questions about your faith and your relationship with God.

Some people want you to believe that asking questions rather than having all the answers is a sign of a weak spirit. I think the opposite is true. Only a person whose spirit is strong and growing can confront obstacles, wrestle with temptation and doubt, and still hold on to faith.

I wish you well on your faith journey. Study, practice, explore, and ask questions. Change and grow. Other seekers will learn from you, and many will follow your lead.

If you ever need a good listener, please call me.

From another seeker,

[YOUR NAME]

First Church   123 Any Street   Your Town, 12345

I Recommend This Young Person

Community Church
12345 Main Street
Anytown, 12345

[DATE]

[NAME AND ADDRESS]

Dear [NAME]:

It is my pleasure to write a letter on behalf of [NAME OF TEENAGER], who is a member of the youth group at [YOUR CHURCH NAME]. It isn't often that I have the opportunity to do something that has absolutely zero degree of difficulty. It is easy to recommend [NAME OF TEENAGER] for [TITLE OR JOB DESCRIPTION].

[NAME OF TEENAGER] is a true leader among [HIS/HER] peers and in our church. When [HE/SHE] accepts a job, we can be sure it will be done well and on time. Adults in the congregation look to [NAME OF TEENAGER] as an example for their own children. Church leaders are challenged by [NAME OF TEENAGER]'s energy and commitment. In other words, [HE/SHE] keeps us all on our toes.

[NAME OF TEENAGER]'s involvement has been extensive and diverse. [INCLUDE SPECIFIC INFORMATION ABOUT TEENAGER'S INVOLVEMENT IN CONGREGATIONAL LIFE.]

I am pleased to give [NAME OF TEENAGER] my wholehearted recommendation. [HIS/HER] presence in your [ORGANIZATION/COMPANY] will be a significant asset.

Please feel free to contact me if you need additional information. And thank you for this opportunity.

Sincerely,

[YOUR NAME]

Parent(s), You Have Great Kids

Your Town Church

[DATE]

[NAME AND ADDRESS]

321 Church Avenue

Anytown,

54321

Dear [NAME]:

I realize it's not in a teenager's job description to tell his or her parents how wonderful they are. I'm writing to make sure you know—you're doing a great job. All of us involved in the youth program at [YOUR CHURCH NAME] appreciate your hard work and terrific results!

It's such a pleasure to have quality young people in our group. It certainly makes my job a joy, so I can understand how much you must appreciate [NAME(S) OF TEENAGER(S)] at home. Great kids don't happen by accident. It's obvious that you've instilled a sense of values into your family and that your expectations are high.

I want you to know how much I appreciate your efforts. Your family is an asset to our program, and it makes me glad to be here! I'm a beneficiary of your hard work.

Thank you!

Sincerely,

[YOUR NAME]

Hey, Volunteer, We Appreciate You

Neighborhood Church   12345 Main Street   Anytown, 12345

[DATE]

[NAME AND ADDRESS]

Dear [NAME]:

I know it's a cliché, but I honestly don't know what our youth ministry program would do without you. If I could pay you, I couldn't pay you enough!

It's a fact: The success of church programs derives more often from the dedication of terrific volunteers than from "wonder-working" staff members. In fact, if there have been any wonderful acts performed in our youth program, you deserve much of the credit.

I'm indebted to you for your generosity of time and energy. You've helped me be successful, and you've contributed to the spiritual and social growth of our young people.

On behalf of them and our entire church, thanks so much for your help. It's a joy to work with you.

Sincerely,

[YOUR NAME]

I Recommend This Volunteer

[DATE]

[NAME AND ADDRESS]

Dear [NAME]:

It's my privilege to write to you and sing the praises of [NAME OF VOLUN-TEER]. While we're sorry to lose such a wonderful worker and volunteer in our youth program at [YOUR CHURCH NAME], we also realize that a treasure is worth much more if it is shared with others.

[NAME OF VOLUNTEER] is a real treasure. Since [HE/SHE] became a volunteer with our youth group, the group has grown in number and spirit. [HE/SHE] has treated [HIS/HER] role as if it were a handsomely salaried position! [NAME OF VOLUNTEER] has always been punctual and dependable. When [HE/SHE] took on a task, [HE/SHE] always followed through and never left loose ends for someone else to pick up. You and I both know how hard it is to find dependable volunteers. [NAME OF VOLUNTEER] is a gem of an exception.

I recommend [NAME OF VOLUNTEER] enthusiastically and without reservation. [HE/SHE] would be a valuable asset to any program that is quality driven. Our loss will truly be your gain if you decide to make [NAME OF VOLUN-TEER] a member of your volunteer staff.

God bless you in your ministry.

Sincerely,

[YOUR NAME]

First Church   123 Any Street   Your Town, 12345

Appeals

Accept Others for Who They Are

Your Town Church

[DATE]

[NAME AND ADDRESS]

321 Church Avenue

Anytown,

54321

Dear [NAME]:

We live in a world where appearances seem to be everything. It's not what you are inside—it's how you look outside. It's not the real you that's important—it's what people think is the real you. We're all too wrapped up in the wrapping around us—instead of the gifts inside us.

You're at a particularly difficult time in your life. You're judged by how you look, but at your age, your body's not even sure what it wants to look like. You lose weight. You gain weight. Your clothes don't fit right. You have two left feet, your hands are too small for your body, and you're growing hair in weird places. Not to mention that zit that's glowing like a laser beam from the middle of your forehead!

Let me remind you of a few things as you live, play, and worship with others. First, treat others with respect and remember that each person is a unique creation of God. Second, look for the real beauty in other people—kindness, integrity, acceptance, and love. Third, stand up and speak out against intolerance and ignorance. Your silence is the same thing as your approval.

Be proud of who you are. I am and so is your church.

Respectfully yours,

[YOUR NAME]

Hey, Group, Let's Stick Together

Neighborhood Church   12345 Main Street   Anytown, 12345

[DATE]

[NAME AND ADDRESS]

Dear [NAME]:

Because our group is going through some tough times right now, I want to encourage everyone to stick together. We've been through a lot. We've leaned on each other through difficult times, and we've hugged each other in triumph. As a family drawn together by love, we can remain strong and overcome the odds.

In life there are many forces that tug at our loyalties. Sometimes false hopes and promises shake our foundation. It's important to know that we can depend on each other during this unsettling time. Right now, we need to support each other and stand firm in our faith.

Let's respect each other's individual differences and tastes without allowing petty disagreements to undermine us.

I'm here if you want to talk. In the meantime, each person in the group is a caretaker of our group's ministry. So take care.

In unity,

[YOUR NAME]

Tell Us Your Opinion

[DATE]

[NAME AND ADDRESS]

Dear [NAME]:

It's healthy to sometimes take a survey of ideas and opinions in a group to find out what members are thinking and feeling. Your responses to this survey will help us make sure our youth ministry program here at [YOUR CHURCH NAME] is on target and meeting your needs. Please be as honest and straightforward as possible; otherwise, this survey will serve little purpose.

Thanks for your honest thoughts and feelings.

[YOUR NAME]

For the following statements, circle the number after each item on a scale of 1 to 5, with 1 representing your total disagreement and 5 representing your total agreement. (Please feel free to share comments on the other side of the survey. You don't have to sign your name.)

1. The youth program here at [YOUR CHURCH NAME] serves my spiritual needs. 1 2 3 4 5

2. The youth program here at [YOUR CHURCH NAME] serves my social needs. 1 2 3 4 5

3. The youth program here at [YOUR CHURCH NAME] serves my recreational needs. 1 2 3 4 5

4. The youth program here at [YOUR CHURCH NAME] is well-balanced and has something for everyone. 1 2 3 4 5

5. I feel loved, accepted, and respected by our youth leaders. 1 2 3 4 5

6. Our youth leaders should provide more leadership. 1 2 3 4 5

7. Our youth leaders should provide less leadership. 1 2 3 4 5

8. The members of our group feel a sense of ownership about the group. 1 2 3 4 5

9. Our pastor takes an active interest in our youth activities. 1 2 3 4 5

10. Our parents take an active interest in our youth activities. 1 2 3 4 5

11. The rest of the church takes an active interest in our youth activities. 1 2 3 4 5

12. I feel like an important part of the church. 1 2 3 4 5

13. My ideas and opinions are valued by our youth leaders. 1 2 3 4 5

14. I feel like an important part of the youth group. 1 2 3 4 5

15. Our youth group is moving forward, growing, and willing to try new things. 1 2 3 4 5

16. Our youth group is open and accepting of all people. 1 2 3 4 5

First Church   **123 Any Street**   **Your Town, 12345**

Parent(s), We Need You

Community Church
12345 Main Street
Anytown, 12345

[DATE]

[NAME AND ADDRESS]

Dear [NAME]:

No group can survive and prosper without the help of willing and active volunteers. [YOUR CHURCH NAME] specifically needs parents who can pitch in and help us with our youth ministry program. Would you be one of those parents?

I know your time is precious and you're already up to your eyebrows in obligations. Without your help, though, we just won't be able to provide the kind of complete youth program that we want to provide for our young people. Our program is growing so quickly that there are just too many hats for the number of heads we have. The more heads we have, the fewer headaches for everyone.

So let's put our heads together and see what kind of helping hands we can come up with. We need chaperones for trips, workers for our events, and helpers for our regular weekly get-togethers. If you're willing to give just a little time, I'll be happy to assign you to something that will fit your schedule.

If you can volunteer some time to our youth program at [YOUR CHURCH NAME], please don't hesitate—call me right now. Thanks!

Sincerely,

[YOUR NAME]

Hey, Volunteer, We Need You

Your Town Church

[DATE]

[NAME AND ADDRESS]

Dear [NAME]:

321 Church Avenue

Anytown,

54321

Would I yell "Fire!" in a crowded theater? Of course not.

Would I yell "Help!" in a crowded room full of teenagers? *Help! Absolutely!* That's why I'm writing this letter.

Over the past several months, our youth program has grown significantly. I'm pleased to tell you that because of our excellent program, our terrific volunteers, and the wonderful support from our church family, our young people—and more of them—*want* to be here.

I want to keep them here, but I need your help. The youth program needs volunteers to make phone calls, flip pancakes, wash dishes, perform taxi service, chaperone outings, participate in worship activities, and just be there—adults to spend just a little of their time to help us maintain a level of excellence.

As our program grows, the need for volunteers grows too. Right now the program is outgrowing our manpower resources. If that trend continues, we may begin to lose momentum, the young people may gradually lose interest, and I might not need to write a letter like this. That would be a sad day for all of us.

Please come forward and lend a hand. The more volunteers we have, the more we can share the work, lightening the load for everyone.

Please call me at [CHURCH PHONE NUMBER]. The youth program needs you!

Sincerely and urgently,

[YOUR NAME]

Hey, Volunteer, We Need Your Opinion

Neighborhood Church 12345 Main Street Anytown, 12345

[DATE]

[NAME AND ADDRESS]

Dear [NAME]:

Since you're such a vital part of our youth ministry program, I value your thoughts and opinions about the health of our program.

We get so busy that we seldom have time to stop and look at what's making us so busy! But for the sake of our kids, we need to take a good look at ourselves.

Would you fill out the enclosed survey (and please be as straightforward as possible)? Thanks for your help and your prompt response on this. We have a great team, and you're definitely a first-string player!

Sincerely,

[YOUR NAME]

Please circle the appropriate number (1, 2, 3, 4, or 5) after each statement, with 1 representing your total agreement and 5 indicating your total disagreement.

1. I feel as if my time with our young people is well-spent.   1   2   3   4   5

2. I feel as if my contribution to the youth program is important.   1   2   3   4   5

3. I feel other leaders appreciate my contribution to the youth program.   1   2   3   4   5

4. I feel the pastor appreciates my contribution to the youth program.   1   2   3   4   5

5. I feel the congregation appreciates my contribution to the youth program.   1   2   3   4   5

6. I feel the teenagers appreciate my contribution to the youth program.   1   2   3   4   5

7. I feel the parents of the teenagers appreciate my contribution to the youth program.   1   2   3   4   5

8. The other youth leaders welcome and value my ideas and opinions.   1   2   3   4   5

9. I am comfortable with the role I have in our youth program.   1   2   3   4   5

10. I am willing and/or able to do more with the youth program if asked.   1   2   3   4   5

11. I believe we need to recruit more volunteers for our youth program.   1   2   3   4   5

12. I have the resources I need to be effective in youth ministry.   1   2   3   4   5

13. As a volunteer, I feel overworked and underappreciated.   1   2   3   4   5

14. I think our staff should spend more time planning and brainstorming.   1   2   3   4   5

15. I believe the pastor(s) needs to be more involved in our staff planning and brainstorming.   1   2   3   4   5

16. I believe our youth program receives great support from our church family.   1   2   3   4   5

17. I think our young people gain a lot from our youth program at [YOUR CHURCH NAME].   1   2   3   4   5

18. I think our youth program includes a good balance of social and spiritual activities.   1   2   3   4   5

Comments:

We Need Drivers

[DATE]

[NAME AND ADDRESS]

Dear [NAME]:

We could call a cab, but that would blow our budget!

Help! We need drivers for [EVENT] at [TIME] on [DATE].

We appreciate the generous support and helping hands that caring adults provide to our young people. Without this help, many of our youth activities would be impossible. When it comes to transportation, we must rely on those of you who (1) have a valid driver's license, (2) can spare the time, and (3) care about providing our young people with interesting and diverse experiences.

I'm hoping that eventually we'll be able to organize a large enough pool of drivers so that we won't have to call on the same people all the time. So we need you, and we also would appreciate your help in recruiting other adults who can help with taxi duty.

Please give me a call at [CHURCH PHONE NUMBER] to volunteer yourself and your vehicle for this important event. We need to have drivers confirmed by no later than [DATE].

Honk if you can help us! And thanks in advance.

Sincerely and for a moving cause,

[YOUR NAME]

First Church **123 Any Street** **Your Town, 12345**

Join Me in Prayer for Our Youth

Community Church
12345 Main Street
Anytown, 12345

[DATE]

[NAME AND ADDRESS]

Dear [NAME]:

I'm writing for your help on a matter of some urgency. Our young people need our prayers as they face the temptations of today's world, which lure them with friendly faces, caring demeanor, and promises of acceptance into the group. It's getting harder and harder to compete with a secular world that views our kids as nothing more than a target market.

I'm concerned, as I know you are, that our kids may not be getting a healthy balance of spiritual food in their diet. With so many parents working and their children going home to empty houses after school, does the intake of secular junk food ever end?

Would you join me at [LOCATION] on [DATE] at [TIME] for a time of prayer for our young people? There is strength in numbers, and I truly believe that the power of collective intercessory prayer for our youth will help keep them on the right track. If we decide this is a worthwhile effort, let's consider making it a regular get-together.

I hope to see you on [DATE] at [TIME] at [LOCATION]. Thank you.

Urgently and prayerfully yours,

[YOUR NAME]

We Need Community Support

Your Town Church

[DATE]

[NAME AND ADDRESS]

321 Church Avenue

Anytown,

54321

Dear [NAME]:

The youth group at [YOUR CHURCH NAME] needs your support for the [EVENT] at [LOCATION] on [DATE] at [TIME].

[YOU MAY WANT TO INCLUDE OTHER DETAILS ABOUT THE EVENT.]

Our community is a caring community, and the young people at [YOUR CHURCH NAME] have always been grateful for the way people rally around worthwhile causes and programs. Your donation of time and material has helped us enrich the lives of others through our various youth ministry outreach programs. Your support has been an investment because it has enabled us to give back to the community.

Once again, we're appealing to your generosity. You can contribute to this program in several ways: [SPECIFIC WAYS THEY CAN HELP].

If you have any questions, please feel free to call me at [CHURCH PHONE NUMBER]. And again, thank you for your help. When it comes right down to it, what preserves us as a caring, sharing community is our mutual respect and support for each other.

Thank you in advance for your interest and support.

Sincerely,

[YOUR NAME]

We Need a Place to Sleep

Neighborhood Church   12345 Main Street   Anytown, 12345

[DATE]

[NAME AND ADDRESS]

Dear [NAME]:

In her poem titled "Up-Hill," Christina Rossetti expresses our hopes exactly:

"Will there be beds for me and all who seek?
Yea, beds for all who come."

The young people at [YOUR CHURCH NAME] will be traveling to [DESTINA-TION] on [DATE]. [YOU MAY WANT TO PROVIDE ADDITIONAL DETAILS ABOUT THE TRIP.] To afford such a venture, we must depend on the kindness of other people. I am writing to find out if you would be willing to poll the families in your congregation to see who would be willing to provide sleeping quarters for one or more of our young people and adult advisors. There will be [NUMBER] female young people and [NUMBER] male young people. We will also have [NUMBER] female adults and [NUMBER] male adults.

The young people have worked long and hard for many months to provide for their needs on this trip. Their meals are already covered. But a few nights of sleeping upright or trying to stretch out on a seat will make us all a little groggy—and we want to be in top form when we reach our destination.

We have sleeping bags. We'll be happy to take a bed, a sofa, a recliner, or even a floor. We will greatly appreciate whatever space your people can provide. We'd like to know by [DATE] if possible.

If you have questions or concerns, or when you have an official bed count, please contact me at [CHURCH PHONE NUMBER].

Thank you for your help and kindness. We look forward to being with you soon.

In anticipation,

[YOUR NAME]

We Need Special Workers for a Special Project

[DATE]

[NAME AND ADDRESS]

Dear [NAME]:

I'm writing to you because you're one of those special workers who constantly reaches beyond your grasp, who always finishes a job, and who leaves behind shoes impossible to fill! In short, this project requires you!

The youth group at [YOUR CHURCH NAME] is organizing a [PROJECT/EVENT] on [DATE] at [TIME]. This is a special opportunity for our young people to shine and for our church to take part in a real ministry.

In order to give you specifics and discuss the various roles that you could play, I would like to ask you to attend a brief brainstorming session at [LOCATION] on [DATE] at [TIME]. At that time, I'll explain the entire project in detail, including the involvement of our young people and the many possibilities for your participation.

Thank you. I hope to see you on [DATE] at [TIME].

Sincerely,

[YOUR NAME]

First Church   123 Any Street   Your Town, 12345

94   Appeals

We Need Support From Our Education Committee/Board/Congregation

Community Church
12345 Main Street
Anytown, 12345

[DATE]

[NAME AND ADDRESS]

Dear [NAME]:

For our youth activities to be successful here at [YOUR CHURCH NAME], we need to have participation by our adult membership. That includes board members, staff, and the entire congregation.

Our young people look to us as examples of commitment and involvement. We can expect them to become active in the work of the church only if we continue to show interest in what they're doing. Also, it's easier to reach beyond our doors and help others if we're reaching out and supporting each other here at [YOUR CHURCH NAME].

You've always been very supportive of our young people. I want you to know how much the young people and their advisors appreciate that. Our young people are here because they feel wanted and needed. But if we allow our support to slacken—if fewer of us volunteer to help with youth projects or if fewer of us attend the youth programs—our young people will begin to feel less important. It's vital that our teenagers continue to feel fully supported by all of us.

I urge you to continue to support the youth activities at [YOUR CHURCH NAME] with your prayers, gifts, and time.

Thank you.

Sincerely,

[YOUR NAME]

Give Us Your Tired, Your Poor... Your Extras

Your Town Church

[DATE]

[NAME AND ADDRESS]

321 Church Avenue

Anytown,

54321

Dear [NAME]:

Let's talk trash—or maybe treasures!

Now is the time to get rid of that gift you (1) never wanted, (2) can't identify, or (3) forgot to give to your spouse last Christmas (and now it doesn't fit)!

This is also an opportunity for you to clean out your garage, attic, basement, closet, and car trunk—and help our youth group, too!

The young people at [YOUR CHURCH NAME] are planning a rummage sale on [DATE] from [START TIME TO FINISH TIME]. [OTHER SPECIFICS MAY BE NECESSARY HERE.] *And we need you to rummage!* We'll take items that have been used hard or hardly used (as long as they still work). We'll even polish 'em up (but you can't have 'em back).

Appliances, apparel (clean and not torn), knickknacks, white elephants—if you don't want it and it can still bring a buck, please donate it to the cause.

All proceeds from the rummage sale will go toward [EVENT/ CAUSE]. We need all items turned in by [DATE]. Just drop off the items at the church, and mark them for the youth rummage sale. If you'd rather have us pick them up, just call [CHURCH PHONE NUMBER], and we'll arrange a pickup time.

Let's talk trash! Call us right now at [CHURCH PHONE NUMBER].

Thanks!

Sincerely,

[YOUR NAME]

We Need Money for a Special Project

Neighborhood Church   12345 Main Street   Anytown, 12345

[DATE]

[NAME AND ADDRESS]

Dear [NAME]:

I won't blame you for thinking, *Oh no—not another fund-raiser!*

But really and truly, this is a project that needs and deserves your support. Please read the following description of the project, and see if you aren't suddenly transformed into a cheerful giver (2 Corinthians 9:7).

[DETAILS ABOUT THE PROJECT, INCLUDING AMOUNT OF MONEY NEEDED.]

Please think seriously about giving whatever you can to this worthy project. Any amount will help us reach our goal. The young people at [YOUR CHURCH NAME] believe this is an opportunity for effective ministry that will make a lasting difference.

When the project is completed, we will provide a report to the entire congregation, detailing our results and any plans for future involvement.

Thank you for your interest and support.

Gratefully yours,

[YOUR NAME]

Please Help Our Youth Group

(to congregation)

[DATE]

[NAME AND ADDRESS]

Dear [NAME]:

Sometimes in the hustle and bustle of church board meetings and planning sessions, our young people get lost in the shuffle. It's important that we remember how much they mean to our church and what they do to help complete the ministry of [YOUR CHURCH NAME].

In a few years, our young people will inherit the responsibility of being care-takers of our church and its many programs. Let me take this opportunity to ask all of you to remember them in your prayers, to support them in their many projects, to contribute your time and money to their programs when-ever possible, and to offer a smile and a pat on the back whenever you come in contact with any of them.

As you know, teenagers, like all of us, will gravitate toward things that inter-est them and people who show interest in them. We must talk to them often and always listen to them.

I hope each of you will be a cheerleader for our young people here at [YOUR CHURCH NAME]. They need to know they're winners!

Thank you.

Sincerely,

[YOUR NAME]

First Church

123 Any Street

Your Town, 12345

Please Pray for Our Youth Group

(to congregation)

Community Church
12345 Main Street
Anytown, 12345

[DATE]

[NAME AND ADDRESS]

Dear [NAME]:

I am writing to ask each of you to remember our young people in your prayers. They need your love and support during this confusing time in their lives.

Writer Quentin Crisp once wrote, "The young always have the same problem—how to rebel and conform at the same time. They have now solved this by defying their parents and copying one another."

Our young people, as wonderful as they are, still act their age most of the time. They want to rebel, and they want to belong. They need to be loved, and they want to be independent. They want to be Christian, and they want to be cool. Sometimes the two are not compatible.

Our kids face temptations every day. I truly believe they face many more negative influences than we did when we were teenagers.

Please accept this as a reminder to remember them in your daily prayers. That alone can make all the difference in their lives.

Sincerely,

[YOUR NAME]

Please Pay Us

Your Town Church

[DATE]

[NAME AND ADDRESS]

321 Church Avenue

Anytown,

54321

Dear [NAME]:

I wanted to thank you again for giving of your resources to help support our youth group here at [NAME OF CHURCH]. It's the generous support of people like you that keeps our ministry going.

I also wanted to remind you that we have not received payment from you in the amount of [AMOUNT] for [SERVICES PERFORMED] on [DATE]. If you have sent it, then please accept my apology, and please call me at [CHURCH PHONE NUMBER] and let me know.

If you've forgotten, please consider this letter a gentle reminder. Our youth program at [YOUR CHURCH NAME] survives because of the kindness and generous support of people like you. Without your help, we would not be able to provide nearly as many programs and services for our kids.

We're all very busy, and I know how easy it is to forget something like this. We thank you again for your contribution and look forward to receiving it soon.

Sincerely,

[YOUR NAME]

Please Come to Our Fund-Raiser

Neighborhood Church   12345 Main Street   Anytown, 12345

[DATE]

[NAME AND ADDRESS]

Dear [NAME]:

The young people at [YOUR CHURCH NAME] are sponsoring a [EVENT] on [DATE] at [TIME] at [LOCATION], and we're asking for your support.

In a word...H-E-L-P!

This year, the youth group plans to participate in several activities that will require additional funding. These activities will also represent significant extensions of our youth ministry outreach.

The funds raised from your support of [NAME OF FUND-RAISER] will go toward [ACTIVITIES OR CAUSES].

The sales pitch is short and simple: We can't do it without your H-E-L-P! Your investment—in the form of your support and participation—will reap returns many times over. Our young people need to experience Christianity in the context of life's many challenges and adventures. Whether it's for a missions trip, a choir tour, summer camp, or a drama production, the funds that make these enrichment opportunities possible must come from a supportive church family.

Please come to [FUND-RAISER] on [DATE] at [TIME] and support youth ministry at [YOUR CHURCH NAME].

H-E-L-P! Thank you.

Sincerely,

[YOUR NAME]

Difficult *Circumstances*

I'm Sorry You Didn't Win the Award

Neighborhood Church   12345 Main Street   Anytown, 12345

[DATE]

[NAME AND ADDRESS]

Dear [NAME]:

I'm so sorry that you didn't receive [NAME OR DESCRIPTION OF AWARD]. I know that a few words from me won't make the disappointment go away—but I sure would like to try to help.

I'm so proud of your accomplishments. I know that your family and church are, too. The fact that you didn't take the top prize doesn't diminish your hard work and tremendous effort.

An award—something you can hold in your hand or hang on your wall —is wonderful. But the work you put into reaching a level not reached by many others has taught you the value of commitment and discipline. That lesson will last you a lifetime—and you'll teach it by example to everyone you touch.

Cheer up! There are many more honors in your future. Ask God for patience and understanding—and continue to do your best.

You're a winner!

Sincerely,

[YOUR NAME]

I'm Sorry About the Death of Your Loved One

[DATE]

[NAME AND ADDRESS]

Dear [NAME]:

Writer John Donne wrote, "Any man's death diminishes me, because I am involved in Mankind."

Your [IDENTITY OF DECEASED] was indeed involved in the lives of so many others who needed a friend. We're all very sad because this is a loss that we all feel deeply.

We're here for you during this difficult time. Lean on us as much as you need to, and let me know if I can be of any help. You'll need time with your family and also by yourself to grieve. Grief is a very necessary part of saying good-bye.

Even during your darkest moments right now, remember that God is with you to help you bear your pain. He is "the Father of compassion and the God of all comfort, who comforts all our troubles" (2 Corinthians 1:3-4a). Remember that through Christ we can have victory over death.

Please accept my sympathies.

[YOUR NAME]

First Church   123 Any Street   Your Town, 12345

I'm Sorry About the Suicide Death of Your Loved One

Community Church
12345 Main Street
Anytown, 12345

[DATE]

[NAME AND ADDRESS]

Dear [NAME]:

I am so sorry to hear about the death of [NAME]. Please accept my deepest sympathies. May you take comfort in Jesus' promise: "Blessed are those who mourn, for they will be comforted" (Matthew 5:4).

Sometimes there is just nothing to say that will ease the pain. This is one of those times; all I can offer is myself as a friend who is praying that God will help you and your loved ones get through this very difficult time. You and I have shared many happy times together. Please know that I share your sorrow right now.

I'm here if you need someone to talk to. I don't want to intrude, but I want you to know that I'm as close as your telephone. You may need some time alone to work through this, but you'll also need to be able to ask for support and to lean on friends who love you.

I'm here. We're all here—when you need us.

Knowing that God will carry you through this,

[YOUR NAME]

I'm Sorry About the Death of Your Parent/Guardian

Your Town Church

321 Church Avenue

Anytown,

54321

[DATE]

[NAME AND ADDRESS]

Dear [NAME]:

Please accept my sympathies on the death of your [MOTHER/ FATHER/GUARDIAN]. Even though [HE/SHE] has left this earthly life, your love for each other remains very much alive.

In that regard, I don't believe any person ever completely dies. Love is still a powerful force in the lives of those who knew and were touched by your [MOTHER/FATHER/ GUARDIAN]. And that love will also continue to shine through you.

At this time, I pray that you will be comforted by God, "the helper of the fatherless" (Psalm 10:14). He is with you as you grieve.

You're in my thoughts and prayers. I'm here if you need me.

God bless you.

[YOUR NAME]

I'm Sorry About the Death of a Youth Group Member

Neighborhood Church   12345 Main Street   Anytown, 12345

[DATE]

[NAME AND ADDRESS]

Dear [NAME]:

This is a sad time for all of us and certainly for [NAME]'s family. Let's remember them in our thoughts. They also need the collective strength and support of our prayers.

We have all suffered a great loss. No one has ever been able to explain why death comes when it does. Even though it's inevitable, death is often unwelcome. But it's a reality of life that all of us must face.

I'm not going to try to explain [NAME]'s death. I don't know why this was [HIS/HER] time to leave us. But I do know that God's timing for our lives, while sometimes shocking and seemingly without reason, is his to determine.

Right now we cry for [NAME]. Our feeling of loss is almost more than we can bear. But what we can gain from this is a clearer understanding of how short our time is together and how precious each one of us is. Because of [NAME]'s death, let's cherish life and each other a little more.

As we grieve over the loss of [NAME], may we look forward to the hope that awaits those who know Christ: "He will lead them to springs of living water. And God will wipe away every tear from their eyes" (Revelation 7:17b).

In celebration of life over death,

[YOUR NAME]

I'm Sorry About the Violent/ Senseless Death in the Community

[DATE]

[NAME AND ADDRESS]

Dear [NAME]:

Sometimes life asks us to deal with the unexplainable, the unacceptable, even the unimaginable. The recent [DESCRIPTION OF VIOLENT ACT] in the news is a supreme test of our faith.

How can good come from tragedy? How can we make sense of the senseless? We can't do it without God's help. We have to ask God to help us find the understanding and grace that it will take for us to get through this tragedy. "The Lord is a refuge for the oppressed, a stronghold in times of trouble" (Psalm 9:9).

"Lord, what can I do to make this world a better place?" is my own personal prayer just now. Think about your personal prayer. Together, through prayer—combined with a commitment to a more active role in society—maybe we can make a difference.

Maybe it starts with saying, "I love you" more often to our family members and friends. Perhaps it's sharing a kind word—or saying, "you matter" with a smile or a nod of the head to people we don't know: *I recognize you as a creation of God—as a person of worth.*

Let's recognize each other today. It's worth our effort.

In Christ,

[YOUR NAME]

First Church   123 Any Street   Your Town, 12345

I'm Sorry About the Death/Loss of Your Pet

Community Church
12345 Main Street
Anytown, 12345

[DATE]

[NAME AND ADDRESS]

Dear [NAME]:

I am so sorry about the loss of your [TYPE OF PET], [NAME OF PET]. The loss of a good friend like [NAME OF PET] can be just as difficult to deal with as the loss of any other loved one.

Writer George Eliot once wrote, "Animals are such agreeable friends— they ask no questions, they pass no criticisms."

It really is rare to find a friend who accepts you just the way you are, without any judging or second-guessing. How sad it is to lose a special friend like that. I hope that even in your grief, you'll remember all the days you shared with [NAME OF PET] and thank God for your time together. So many people never experience the joy of that kind of special friendship. *You have*—and that makes you very lucky!

Please accept my sympathies. I can't pretend to be able to fix the hurt you feel, but I am here if you need someone to talk to or need a shoulder to lean on during your sadness.

Sincerely yours,

[YOUR NAME]

I'm Sorry About the Loss of Your Job

Your Town Church

[DATE]

[NAME AND ADDRESS]

321 Church Avenue

Anytown,

Dear [NAME]:

54321

I'm so sorry to hear that you lost your job. First, let me encourage you to use me as a reference or to have me write a letter of recommendation for you, if either will help.

Losing a job can make you feel pretty low, no matter if you were fired, you were laid off, or you just decided it was time for a change. Ask God to help you keep a positive outlook.

The job that you had is now in the past. It's important that you keep your head up and aim higher than before. Do your homework, talk to friends and neighbors, look through the "help wanted" ads—go after something that will challenge you and perhaps lay the foundation for a solid career. Ask God for guidance.

When you lose a job, you have two choices. You can let it knock you down for the count—or you can stay on your feet, flex your muscle, and come out a winner! I'm confident you'll make the right choice.

Keep your faith in God—and have faith in yourself. Let me know how I can help.

Sincerely,

[YOUR NAME]

I'm Sorry About the Loss of Your Parent's Job

Neighborhood Church   12345 Main Street   Anytown, 12345

[DATE]

[NAME AND ADDRESS]

Dear [NAME]:

I'm so sorry that your [MOTHER/FATHER/GUARDIAN] lost [HIS/HER] job. That seems to be the plight of so many people these days—no matter how hard they work and how loyal they are to their employers.

While life right now may not seem very fair to you, we want you to know that your many friends are thinking of you. The youth group at [YOUR CHURCH NAME] and I would like to help and support you in any way we can.

What can we do to help? Does your family need baby-sitting services? someone to do grocery shopping? someone to type and make copies of a résumé? someone to provide transportation? help with lawn care? help with cooking? We can't find your [MOTHER/FATHER/GUARDIAN] a new job, but we can sure help ease the workload at home to make job hunting a little easier.

Call me at [PHONE NUMBER(S)]. We're here to help, but we don't want to be in the way. I'll wait to hear from you—and *please* don't hesitate to ask!

Sincerely,

[YOUR NAME]

Why a Youth Leader Is Leaving

(follow-up letter to young people)

[DATE]

[NAME AND ADDRESS]

Dear [NAME]:

Sometimes life hits us right between the eyes with a real disappointment. The fact that [DEPARTING YOUTH LEADER] is leaving us makes us all want to scream, pull our hair, or just quietly shake our heads.

It's important that we go on from here and continue to build our program. For a while, we'll all feel empty or hurt, but a program's strength has to be built on the efforts of everyone, not on just one person. No one needs to feel any fault or place any blame. The situation, even though it's unpleasant, is one of those detours in life that we must get around. And together we will.

We will continue to care about [DEPARTING YOUTH LEADER] and remember [HIS/HER] contributions. Let's also remember [HIM/HER] in our prayers and ask God to keep our ministry strong and on course.

Sincerely,

[YOUR NAME]

First Church

123 Any Street

Your Town, 12345

Why I'm Leaving

(follow-up letter to young people)

Community Church
12345 Main Street
Anytown, 12345

[DATE]

[NAME AND ADDRESS]

Dear [YOUR CHURCH NAME] youth group:

We've spent many wonderful times together, and you'll enjoy many more experiences as a youth group. You're very special people to me, and I know some of you may feel disappointed because I'm resigning my position as your youth leader. I hope you're able to understand my reasons as I've tried to explain them to you. This change is necessary and good.

I've appreciated your dedication and hard work to help make our group successful. Some of you have matured in your faith through your friendships with each other. You've struggled with social and spiritual issues, and you've been able to keep God first in your lives. I'm proud of all of you for putting the interests of the group ahead of personal desires. The group is strong because of your commitment to its mission and purpose.

This ministry at [YOUR CHURCH NAME] needs you now more than ever. Nurture it, build it, and welcome others into it.

I'll keep you in my prayers. Thanks for being part of my life. You'll always be important to me.

Sincerely,

[YOUR NAME]

Please Stop Your Disruptive Behavior
(follow-up letter)

Your Town Church

321 Church Avenue

Anytown,

54321

[DATE]

[NAME AND ADDRESS]

Dear [NAME]:

Some letters are just no fun at all, and this is one of them. But it's important for us to review our recent conversation and come to some kind of understanding.

[FIRST NAME OF TEENAGER], I want you to be part of our youth group. I want you to participate, have fun, and make new friends. I also happen to believe that the others will benefit from getting to know you. I believe all of this can happen if you make the decision to contribute to the group in a constructive way.

I've always believed that our doors need to be open to anyone who wants to be part of our youth program. But when one person's presence turns a program or activity into a negative experience for everyone else, I have to consider what to do for the good of the entire group.

I want you to be part of our fellowship. The key phrase, though, is *part of*—joining in group activities and discussion in positive ways.

Let's get together and talk again before the next youth gathering, on [DATE]. Please call me at [PHONE NUMBER] to arrange a time—or if I don't hear from you in the next couple of days, I'll be happy to call you.

I hope we can come to some understanding so this can still be a matter just between you and me.

Thank you.

With concern,

[YOUR NAME]

I'm Temporarily Suspending You

(follow-up letter to a youth group member)

Neighborhood Church   12345 Main Street   Anytown, 12345

[DATE]

[NAME AND ADDRESS]

Dear [NAME]:

This is to follow up on our recent conversation about your involvement in the youth group at [YOUR CHURCH NAME] and my request that you not attend any more group activities for a time.

First, [NAME OF TEENAGER], you're important to me. I care about you and love you as one of God's wonderful creations. Second, I want you to know that my hope and prayer is for you to be able to return to the group and be a part of a loving, caring community.

During your absence from the group, you need to think about (1) the purpose of our youth program and (2) your reasons for attending. When you decide to return to the group, you and I will need to discuss these issues. I will want to talk with you about why you're ready to come back to the group and how you're planning to change your behavior. If you're ready to do both, I'll be the first to welcome you back with open arms.

[NAME OF TEENAGER], you can be a very positive force in our group if you choose to be. I hope your time away from us will help you make that choice. When you're ready to talk about this some more, please let me know. In the meantime, I'll stay in touch with you. I know we can come up with a plan for working this out together.

With high hopes,

[YOUR NAME]

Difficult Circumstances

You Have My Support and Acceptance
(pregnant teenager)

[DATE]

[NAME AND ADDRESS]

Dear [NAME]:

I'm writing this letter to offer you my help and support throughout this difficult time in your life.

First of all, I want you to know, [FIRST NAME OF TEENAGER], that I am not interested in making any judgments or accusations. I'm sure you're experiencing some of that already. Those kinds of reactions—from both friends and family—are part of the reality of your situation.

Try to understand that those who know you—even those who love you—may be shocked, a little hurt, and maybe disappointed. That doesn't necessarily mean they won't be there when you need them. Even the most important people in your life will need some time to work through this.

I don't want to interfere, but I'd like to share some personal thoughts. Blame is destructive, so try not to place any on yourself or anyone else. It takes courage, though, to assume responsibility for your situation.

Accept help and support from those who know and love you. You'll know who they are. It would be a mistake for you to try to deal with this alone. It wouldn't be fair to yourself, your loved ones, or that special little person on the way.

This kind of situation sometimes brings out the best and the worst in people. So my final word to you is to simply ask God for strength, courage, and the ability to forgive those who will be quick to judge you.

Now is the time to let go of the past and be positive about your future. I'm here if you need a friend. Feel free to call me or knock on my door.

Sincerely,

[YOUR NAME]

First Church   **123 Any Street**   **Your Town, 12345**

You Have My Support and Acceptance

(soon-to-be teenage father)

Community Church
12345 Main Street
Anytown, 12345

[DATE]

[NAME AND ADDRESS]

Dear [NAME]:

I'd like to offer my help and support as you and [NAME OF FEMALE] face this new challenge together—bringing a new life into the world.

I emphasize the word *together*, [NAME OF MALE TEENAGER], because I hope and pray that you will remain an active partner in this and give your love and support to [NAME OF FEMALE]. Without making any judgments, I encourage you—with God's guidance—to take hold of your responsibility.

Try to understand that those who know you—even those who love you—may be shocked, a little hurt, and perhaps disappointed. That doesn't necessarily mean they won't be there when you need them. Even the most important people in your life will need some time to work through this.

I don't want to interfere, but I'd like to share some personal thoughts. Blame is destructive, so try not to place any on yourself or anyone else. It takes courage, though, to assume responsibility for your situation.

Accept help and support from those who know and love you. You'll know who they are. It would be a mistake for you and [NAME OF FEMALE] to try to deal with this alone. It wouldn't be fair to yourselves, your loved ones, or that special little person on the way.

Finally, turn this situation over to God and ask him for strength, courage, and the ability to forgive. Some people may already be pointing accusing fingers at you. Be prepared for that—and find room in your heart to forgive them just as you want them to forgive you.

[NAME OF TEENAGER], now is the time to let go of the past and be positive about your future. I'm here if you need a friend. Just call me or knock on my door.

Sincerely,

[YOUR NAME]

May You Be Healed From Your Terminal Illness

Your Town Church

321 Church Avenue

Anytown,

54321

[DATE]

[NAME AND ADDRESS]

Dear [NAME]:

"For my Father's will is that everyone who looks to the Son and believes in him shall have eternal life, and I will raise him up at the last day" (John 6:40).

Jesus spoke those words to a crowd of people who were following him from place to place. Many were hungry for his words of assurance.

Let me add my own words of assurance as I struggle to find the right ones to say. You're in the thoughts and prayers of all of us who know and love you—who are fortunate enough to call you *friend*. Dear friend, we pray for the miracle of your healing.

I believe in miracles. I pray that your body will be touched by God's healing hand. But I also know that our Creator allows life to happen to us. Part of that life is death—and we have his promise that for those who know Christ, our earthly death is just a passageway to a new life with him.

I thank God for your life. You have touched us all and made a difference.

In prayer for your healing,

[YOUR NAME]

I'm Sorry Your Parents Are Separating/Divorcing

Neighborhood Church   12345 Main Street   Anytown, 12345

[DATE]

[NAME AND DATE]

Dear [NAME]:

I realize that the difficulties your parents are going through right now are creating anxiety and confusion for you and your family. I want you to know that I'm here if you need someone to talk to or just to listen.

It's important that you know, [NAME], that you're not responsible for your parents splitting up. Also, you don't need to carry your hurt all by yourself. You have many friends here at [YOUR CHURCH NAME] who are ready to help you through this tough time.

Hang in there. Pray for your mom and dad. Ask God to heal their wounds, and love them both as much as you can. They'll need your love because believe it or not, both of them will hurt inside for a long time.

Remember—the invitation to talk is always open. I understand if you want some time to yourself, so I'll step back and let you make the first contact. *Please* don't hesitate.

Sincerely,

[YOUR NAME]

Disk File #104

Get Well
(illness)

[DATE]

[NAME AND ADDRESS]

Dear [NAME]:

The whole gang at [YOUR CHURCH NAME] would like you to know that we're praying for your speedy recovery.

We've decided that your illness is God's way of reminding us all to slow down, get more rest, and take time to smell the flowers. So we're slowing down, getting more rest, and sniffing every flower in sight! *We feel terrific!* Thanks for the inspiration.

We've even come up with some jokes to cheer you up! Here they are:

Did you know that Moses was sick a lot?
Yep, he suffered from a chronic Sinai condition.

Your being sick reminded us of the parable of the lost sheep.
Missing ewe! (Are you laughing yet?)

We have one more—hope it doesn't cause a relapse:

Last Sunday the pastor played the role of a circuit rider.
You missed a great sermon on the mount! (Do we need to explain it?)

Well, we're happy that we cheered you up—or should we apologize? Anyway, we miss you, and we can't wait for you to come back. Take it slow—but get better fast! Since you've been gone, we've appointed you to four committees—and you're already way behind!

We'll visit soon! We love you.

[YOUR NAME]

First Church 123 Any Street **Your Town, 12345**

Get Well

(injury from accident)

Community Church
12345 Main Street
Anytown, 12345

[DATE]

[NAME AND ADDRESS]

Dear [NAME]:

Hey, it's exciting enough just to know you—you didn't need to cause this much drama!

The whole gang sends their best wishes for a speedy recovery. We're just thankful your injuries aren't any worse.

You sure missed a great sermon last Sunday. The pastor talked about a couple of dreams he'd had lately. Friday night he dreamed he was a tepee. Saturday night he dreamed he was a wigwam. We all decided we know what the problem is—*he's two tents!* (Ba-dum-dum!)

Also, they asked the youth group to take the offering. I thought that was a really nice thing to do. The next day we had to give it back—of all the nerve! (Don't laugh too hard—you'll fall outta bed!)

How about some Bible trivia? What was it that a Roman soldier dared not hide in his closet? Give up? A pair of Levites! If Noah had it to do all over again, what would he have taken with him? *Air freshener*, of course!

Well, good friend, in order that there be some hope for your recovery, we'll stop. Our thoughts and prayers are with you, and we're looking forward to your return. The faster you get back here, the less you'll have to put up with our sick humor! (Although we've saved a few for when we come to visit.)

Godspeed in your healing. We love you.

[YOUR NAME]

Parent(s), Your Teenager Is Disruptive

Your Town Church

[DATE]

[NAME AND ADDRESS]

321 Church Avenue

Anytown,

54321

Dear [NAME]:

This kind of letter is never easy to write, but I know that as a concerned parent you would want me to write it. It is in [NAME OF TEENAGER]'s best interest that I do so.

I need your help. Perhaps you can shed some light on why [NAME OF TEENAGER] is increasingly disruptive during our youth gatherings. I fully realize that at [HIS/HER] age young people face many pressures and expectations. Often those things manifest themselves in negative behavior. Right now, [HE/SHE] is exhibiting uncharacteristically poor judgment and bad manners. I've had to exclude [HIM/HER] from some activities during our group time in order to have an orderly session.

I don't wish to exclude anyone from our activities. [NAME OF TEENAGER], like the others in the group, needs the support and fellowship that the group offers. I can't relate effectively to everyone, though, when the poor behavior of a few takes up all my time. It would distress me to have to ask [NAME OF TEENAGER] not to attend our youth activities, and with your help, I hope it won't come to that.

I would be grateful if we could speak to [NAME OF TEENAGER] together and help [HIM/HER] understand the consequences of [HIS/HER] actions. Please call me if you think we can work together to help [NAME OF TEENAGER] through this unsettling time.

Thank you for your understanding and concern.

Sincerely concerned,

[YOUR NAME]

Goodbye, Volunteer
(leaving the group)

Neighborhood Church   12345 Main Street   Anytown, 12345

[DATE]

[NAME AND ADDRESS]

Dear [NAME]:

What in the world will we do without you? I suppose your family would notice you were gone if we kidnapped you and kept you in the church basement. I guess we'll have to let you go—at least for a while.

Your dedication to our youth group has been extraordinary. While we'll never be able to replace you, the group will continue to prosper because of the time and energy you gave to it. We'll carry on in the tradition of excellence that you helped establish.

If, following a rest from the rigors of car washes, pancake breakfasts, hayrides, and other good clean pandemonium, you find that you miss us horribly, we'll be glad to have you back!

Thank you for sharing your time with us. God bless you.

With our thanks,

[YOUR NAME]

Goodbye, Volunteer
(leaving the church)

[DATE]

[NAME AND ADDRESS]

Dear [NAME]:

What in the world will we do without you? We can't kidnap you and keep you in the church basement. We can't bribe you or blackmail you. We can't clone you. (If only we could!)

Well, I'll tell you what we'll do without you: Because you leave behind a legacy of excellence and achievement with our group, we'll do everything we did before. It may not be as easy without you, but we'll have your example to follow.

We're all going to miss you so much. You've shared your life with us, and we truly are richer for it. Thank you for all you've done and what you've meant to us. I know we're not suppose to be envious, but those folks in your future sure are lucky!

You've made many wonderful friends here, especially among our young people. They will surely continue to grow in Christ because of your car-ing, loving touch.

Thanks for sharing you with us. We love you.

Sincerely,

[YOUR NAME]

First Church   **123 Any Street**   **Your Town, 12345**

Please Resign Your Position

(follow-up letter to a volunteer)

Community Church
12345 Main Street
Anytown, 12345

[DATE]

[NAME AND ADDRESS]

Dear [NAME]:

Those of us who work on the church staff thank God every day for volunteers, without whom we couldn't get it all done. Sometimes we have to ask God for strength when we have the unpleasant duty of removing a volunteer from a specific task.

[NAME OF VOLUNTEER], I know our recent conversation and decision have been difficult for both of us. I wish there were a less painful way (for both of us) to deal with it. But it's difficult to preserve our relationship if we can't be honest with each other.

A willing volunteer needs to love what [HE/SHE] is doing. In that regard, you fill the bill. And I'm sure your love for our church and its programs will be put to good use in an area more suited to your abilities.

[NAME OF VOLUNTEER], I pray that this incident will not end our friendship. Perhaps time away from the youth program will give you a fresh perspective on where your talents can be better utilized.

I pray that you will understand my position.

With regret and respect,

[YOUR NAME]

I'm Resigning
(to officials)

Your Town Church

[DATE]

[NAME AND ADDRESS]

321 Church Avenue

Anytown,

54321

Dear [NAME]:

It is with great regret that I write this letter to inform you of my resignation as youth leader at [YOUR CHURCH NAME], effective [DATE].

This role has changed my life over the past [AMOUNT OF TIME]. My work with our young people could hardly be called work at all—they have gifted my life with purpose, challenge, humor, and feelings that no words can capture. We are fortunate to have such a terrific group of young people. The future of [YOUR CHURCH NAME] is assured—it will rest in capable hands.

I have prayed about this decision, and I truly believe it is the right thing to do. Let me share my reasons.

[PROVIDE REASONS BASED ON SPECIFIC CIRCUMSTANCES.]

I want to thank you for this opportunity to work with the young people at [YOUR CHURCH NAME]. They are our greatest assets, and I encourage everyone to continue to listen to them, talk to them, work with them, cheer for them, and—most of all—pray for them.

If I can be of assistance in hiring a replacement, please don't hesitate to ask. I am extremely interested in seeing that my successor is nothing short of magnificent. Our kids deserve nothing less.

Thank you for your understanding and for the privilege of serving the young people of [YOUR CHURCH NAME].

Sincerely,

[YOUR NAME]

Alphabetical Index

Topical Index